Girl Seeks Bliss

ZEN AND
THE ART OF
MODERN LIFE
MAINTENANCE

Girl Seeks Bliss

ZEN AND
THE ART OF
MODERN LIFE
MAINTENANCE

NICOLE BELAND

A PLUME BOOK

PLUME
Published by Penguin Group
Penguin Group (USA) Inc., 375 Hudson Street, New York, New York 10014, U.S.A.
Penguin Group (Canada), 10 Alcorn Avenue, Toronto, Ontario, Canada M4V 3B2
(a division of Pearson Penguin Canada Inc.)
Penguin Books, Ltd., 80 Strand, London WC2R 0RL, England
Penguin Ireland, 25 St. Stephen's Green, Dublin 2, Ireland
(a division of Penguin Books Ltd.)
Penguin Group (Australia), 250 Camberwell Road, Camberwell, Victoria 3124, Australia
(a division of Pearson Australia Group Pty. Ltd.)
Penguin Books India Pvt. Ltd., 11 Community Centre, Panchsheel Park,
New Delhi – 100 017, India
Penguin Books (NZ), cnr Airborne and Rosedale Roads, Albany, Auckland 1310,
New Zealand (a division of Pearson New Zealand Ltd.)
Penguin Books (South Africa) (Pty.) Ltd., 24 Sturdee Avenue, Rosebank,
Johannesburg 2196, South Africa

Penguin Books Ltd., Registered Offices: 80 Strand, London WC2R 0RL, England

First published by Plume, a member of Penguin Group (USA) Inc.

First Printing, June 2005
10   9   8   7   6   5   4   3   2   1

Ⓟ REGISTERED TRADEMARK—MARCA REGISTRADA

LIBRARY OF CONGRESS CATALOGING-IN-PUBLICATION DATA

Beland, Nicole.
    Girl seeks bliss : Zen and the art of modern life maintenance / Nicole Beland.
        p. cm.
    Summary: Fundamental concepts of Buddhism for the modern-day woman.
    ISBN 0-452-28577-1
    1. Religious life—Buddhism.   2. Buddhism—Doctrines.   I. Title.
    BQ4302.B45 2005
    294.3'444'082—dc22

                                                                    2004026566

Printed in the United States of America
Set in Optima
Designed by Eve L. Kirch

Author's Note

This book contains the fundamental concepts of Buddhism as I—a humble Buddhist scholar—have come to understand them through the books that I've read and the lectures and classes that I've attended. As with any religion, people all over the world have their own interpretations of specific tenets and practices of Buddhism. If you have a deepening interest in this wise and simple yet extremely profound way of life, I urge you to continue doing your own research through the many books and Web sites available, some of which are listed in these pages.

Hoping to call attention to their wish for world peace, a Buddhist monk and one of his students spent two years and nine months walking eight hundred miles on their way from Los Angeles to a town in northern California called The City of Ten Thousand Buddhas. They set out in May of 1977 and moved at the speed of three steps and one bow the entire way. With their hands held in prayer position in front of their hearts, they took three mindful strides and then knelt down, placed their foreheads on the ground, and sent out a message of peace to every living thing on the planet. Then they rose up into standing position and started again. No matter what happened on their journey—some people cheered them on, others threw rocks and garbage at them—they just kept walking and bowing, emanating peace and love every inch of the way.

ACKNOWLEDGMENTS

My deepest thanks to John Zeman, Jenai and Saul Cohen, Evon and Omer Beland, Allison Schwartz, Liesa Goins, and Florian Bachleda for their love, friendship, and endless support; Katharine Cluverius for her wise guidance in all things literary; and Julie Saltman for believing in this book and providing insightful suggestions every step of the way.

CONTENTS

INTRODUCTION

High up in the mountains of Nepal there lies a solitary cave where you or I could meditate for half a dozen years, slowly boring a hole into the stone wall with our unwavering gaze until we fully realize the nature of the universe—the result of which would be a level of bliss so complete (aka *nirvana*), we'd have a serene "Buddha smile" plastered on our face for all of eternity. If we were Buddhist monks, entirely focused on becoming enlightened, that's probably what we'd do. But we're not monks—not even close—and for a very good reason: the everyday world and all of its pleasure and passion is far too fun and intriguing to leave behind (or, I should say, rise above). So maybe we'll never become twenty-first century Buddhas, but we *can* come a lot closer to achieving the kind of satisfaction and happiness that this spiritual revolutionary attained twenty-five hundred years ago.

Ever since stumbling across Shunryu Suzuki's classic *Zen Mind, Beginner's Mind* in my parents' bookcase when I was seventeen (my half-Chinese, half-Indian mother has always been interested in Eastern wisdom), I've been working my way through dozens of books by monks, nuns, academics, and meditation teachers. And the more I've learned about Buddhism, the more convinced I am that Buddha's simple, logical advice is some of the most intelligent and useful out there. Now in my early thirties, I continue to be surprised at how much it helps me get through my often stressful and always unpredictable life (I'm a freelance journalist living in New York—which means no job security, sky-high credit card bills, too much partying, too little time to exercise or eat right, and never enough sleep).

I don't consider myself a practicing Buddhist (mostly because I don't like to think of myself as a practicing *anything*), but there's no doubt that Buddhism has a powerful and positive influence on me every minute of every day, no matter what I'm doing or who I'm with. It's made me calmer, happier, and infinitely more content with who I am and with life in general (no easy feat, given what's happening in this often violent and unfair world). It's also helping me become a more generous and understanding friend, girlfriend, sister, and daughter.

Until recently, I was one of few people browsing the Eastern Philosophy section of the bookstore who wasn't wearing hemp or emitting the scent of patchouli. But the scene is changing dramatically. These days, I'm bumping elbows with a crowd of yoga-loving women who, like me, are determined to attain a more profound sense of well-being than can be found at the gym, at the mall, at work, or even in our personal relationships. Twenty- and thirty-somethings in designer jeans and stiletto heels are also packing the weekly meditation classes I attend at a Buddhist center run by Uma Thurman's dad, an ordained monk and professor of Tibetan culture at Columbia University. My favorite teacher there, Noah Levine, is an ex–punk rocker who rides a motorcycle and is covered in tattoos. This is definitely *not* your hippie uncle's idea of Buddhism.

You've most likely picked up this book because you're curious about Buddhism and are hoping to achieve a more gratifying state of bliss on a daily basis. I'm so glad you did, and I hope that the following pages will provide exactly what you're looking for.

1

Life According to Buddha

You could say that Buddha was a kind of spiritual Einstein—a think-outside-the-box intellectual who decided to focus his efforts on understanding and overcoming the fundamental causes of human unhappiness. Some time around 450 BC his study led to breakthroughs about the nature of existence. Those breakthroughs form the basis of Buddhism, and they still stand up to scrutiny some twenty-five hundred years later.

Contrary to what the robes, temples, and rituals might lead you to believe, Buddhism doesn't have much in common with most other major religions. For one thing, there is no all-knowing, all-powerful deity to worship, please, or piss off. Buddha never claimed to be a god or to believe in any gods. As far as rewards and punishments for everyday actions go, he taught that if a person acts *skillfully*—with intelligence and compassion—good things are likely to come her way. If a person acts *unskillfully*—with ignorance and carelessness—then it's likely that her life will often be difficult and unpleasant. He considered this to be a natural, universal law.

Buddhism in its most basic form—stripped of the different cultural traditions that have risen around it over the centuries—is best described as a type of secular logic that anyone is free to agree or disagree with. That's why so many practical, realistic people are

3

attracted to it. Buddha taught that the only way to know anything for sure was to experience it yourself. So he advised his students to put his ideas to the test before deciding if they were true. As for far-out questions such as where all life comes from or what happens when we die, his standpoint was that while they were fine subjects to ruminate on, getting all riled up over the unknowable is no way to free ourselves from suffering and enjoy life from moment to moment. For people who are looking for a straightforward, no-bullshit approach to happiness, Buddhism is one big breath of fresh air.

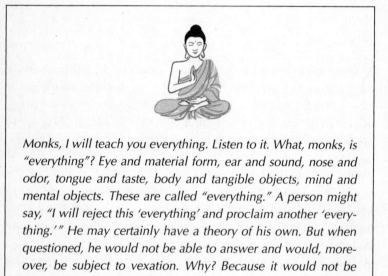

Monks, I will teach you everything. Listen to it. What, monks, is "everything"? Eye and material form, ear and sound, nose and odor, tongue and taste, body and tangible objects, mind and mental objects. These are called "everything." A person might say, "I will reject this 'everything' and proclaim another 'everything.'" He may certainly have a theory of his own. But when questioned, he would not be able to answer and would, moreover, be subject to vexation. Why? Because it would not be within the range of experience.

BUDDHIST LOGIC 101

At the very core of every school of Buddhism around the world are *the four noble truths.* Buddha came to these four conclusions about how the world works after years of education, personal experience, and meditation.

Noble Truth #1

The first noble truth is that life isn't easy for anyone. Regardless of how gorgeous, rich, talented, brilliant, funny, or popular a person may be, she will often be unhappy, unsatisfied, confused, angry, lonely, uncomfortable, nervous, and every other negative emotion you can think of. Supermodels, Oscar-winning actresses, ridiculously rich heiresses—they will all curl up in their beds, cry their hearts out, and feel like crap countless times over the course of their lives. This is because there is no such thing as lasting satisfaction or never-ending happiness for anyone. Nothing is permanent, not the the good or the bad. That might sound like a downer, but it doesn't have to be. Reminding ourselves that everyone struggles with the same disappointments, fears, and anxieties has a way of making our own problems feel a little less dramatic and a lot easier to bear. That's why picking up the phone and telling a friend all about some disaster in your life is such a relief. You get it all off of your chest and she reminds you that something like that once happened to her. She gets it. She knows what you're going through. She feels your pain. That simple compassion is usually enough to calm us down.

Understanding that absolutely everyone suffers at one point or another also sucks the life right out of envy and jealousy. We might think we'd be happier if we were all world-class athletes with PhDs and a billion dollars in the bank, but who knows what the downsides of that life would be? Maybe they would be harder to take than your current reality (I know it's hard to imagine, but consider the behind-the-scenes lives of Marilyn Monroe or Princess Diana). Most importantly, realizing that negative emotions and events are an inherent part of life is the first step to overcoming them. If we even begin to accept the first noble truth—**suffering is a natural part of existence**—then suffering itself loses some of its power over us.

Desperately Seeking Siddhartha

If you were looking for Buddha in a crowded room, you'd do best to keep your eye out for a six-foot-tall Indian guy with blue eyes and a suspiciously serene smile. Those are the few physical characteristics of the sage that are consistently backed by various sources. As with any other larger-than-life figure who existed prior to photography, Buddha's image has been interpreted and embellished by artists from different cultures, who often gave him traits they considered superior to the average guy (extra long earlobes, hair that curled only in one direction, an enormous penis, webbed fingers and toes, that massive spare tire and those jolly cheeks . . .).

Historians agree that the Buddha was born Siddhartha Gautama around 543 BC in what is now the western part of Nepal. His parents belonged to the Kshatriya caste, the second highest in the Indian class system and the one responsible for running the military and government. Siddhartha's father was the king of his clan (called the Sakyas), making his mother a queen and Siddhartha a bona fide prince. He was married around the age of seventeen to one of his equally well-off cousins (getting hitched as a teen and to a distant family member were both common practices at the time). He probably had many children with his wife and concubines, one of which was a son named Rahula, who later became a devoted follower.

If the Buddha were alive today he'd probably have a triple PhD in philosophy, religion, and psychology and a tenured position at Harvard, though he wouldn't have focused on those subjects until he was around thirty years old. As the story goes, it was at that point in his life that he decided to start investigating the causes of human suffering. He was an eager and tireless student. Before devising his own route to happiness, he explored several established intellectual and spiritual paths, including a form of asceticism that involved near-starvation and total exposure to the elements. After seven years of studying with philosophers and religious leaders, he finally had the breakthrough that allowed him to understand life on a deeper level. That breakthrough, which occurred after fasting and meditating for several days, was his realization of nirvana. From then on he was known as the Buddha, or *awakened one.*

Noble Truth #2

The second noble truth is that **suffering is caused by unnecessary craving**. To some extent, that includes the small stuff—vanilla chai lattés, Prada shoes, a smaller laptop, a pair of jeans that make your ass look perfect. We think, *If only I had that right now, I'd be happy.* Which we are, for a few minutes here and there. But superficial acquisitions don't provide deep satisfaction, or prevent us from feeling sad, lonely, lost, or frustrated. We forget about them soon after we have them and start jonesing for something else. While craving the little stuff can drain our bank accounts and waste a lot of our time and energy, it usually leads to only a mild amount of suffering. Most of us don't get too bent out of shape if we can't get our hands on a particular shade of red lipstick. It's the serious, deep-seated cravings that really make us inconsolable—wishing that a relationship wasn't ending, that we could take back something regrettable that we did or said in the past, that we had a different job, a different body, a different life. These kinds of cravings can make us seriously depressed. Wanting things, people, or emotions to stay as they are is another kind of wishful thinking that gets us into major trouble, as is the desire to completely control another person or a situation. The second noble truth is crucial to Buddhism because we have to know what makes us unhappy in order to defeat it.

Noble Truth #3

Now, finally, comes the ray of sunshine: *the third noble truth* states simply that **there is a way to reduce, and even end, suffering**. Instead of waiting for those rare, wonderful flashes of calm satisfaction to occur at random, we can train ourselves to feel more content on a regular basis. For those of us whose goal is not to become a fully devoted Buddhist monk who spends the great majority of her time meditating, it's unlikely that we'll ever feel completely impervious to all of the annoyances and difficulties of daily life. But just beginning to embrace Buddhist philosophy can help us keep each glitch in perspective, bounce back more quickly, and handle the whole messy struggle with a lot more patience and grace.

Noble Truth #4

So, exactly how long and complicated is the Buddha's path to happiness? Not long or complicated—but definitely not easy. *The fourth noble truth* consists of **eight basic guidelines for living the good life, otherwise known as the eightfold path.** As with every other aspect of his teaching, Buddha insisted that any interested person test his theories for herself and never take for granted that they're right or true. So consider the following eight bits of advice to be exactly that: advice, not rules. These ideas are ancient, but as wise and practical as ever. Keep in mind that Buddha conveyed all of the nuances of his philosophy orally between the years of 490 BC and 450 BC. It wasn't until centuries later that his teachings—which had been memorized and passed on from one generation of monks to the next—were written down in Sanskrit and Pali, an ancient Indo-Aryan dialect, and eventually translated into English. As a result, there is a lot of human interpretation involved here—including my own. All that matters is what rings true to you.

THE EIGHTFOLD PATH

STEP 1: *Right Understanding*

This first step of the path is about opening our eyes and perceiving the world as it is, rather than as we might expect, hope, or fear it will be. Have you ever thought that you had Coke in your glass and then took a sip and nearly jumped out of your skin because it turned out to be lemonade or iced tea or whatever else? That's how strongly our expectations influence our responses. Expectations—whether they're positive or negative—are a huge cause of everyday suffering. They distort what we see and hear and make it incredibly difficult to approach an experience with clarity or openness.

A typical way in which our expectations cause problems is when we become dead set on things going exactly as we want them to. We plan like mad, double-check the details, and make sure that absolutely nothing can go wrong. Of course, by wrong, we just mean different from the fantasy that we've created in our heads. Inevitably, something doesn't match up with that fantasy—the only table available in the restaurant is next to the bathroom, the people sitting next to you are loud and obnoxious, the new shoes you're wearing are ripping the skin off of your toes, your date is in a bad mood. As a result, you feel disappointed—and disappointment is a particularly nasty form of suffering. But, with a little effort, it can be avoided most of the time.

Part of attaining *right understanding* is realizing how expectations can and do make our lives much more difficult. While it's OK to plan or think ahead, it's never a good idea to convince ourselves that things are guaranteed to be one way or the other. When we stay open to the theory that whatever happens happens, we feel less vulnerable and more at ease. Things don't upset us so easily. I'll talk more about that in the next chapter, which is all about taking things in stride.

Right understanding also requires that we ponder three basic ideas about life, known as *the three marks of existence*:

Impermanence—Nothing is this world is fixed or unchanging—no thing, no thought, no emotion. Because of this, it is pointless to try to grasp, or hold on to anything material or immaterial. Instead, we should be open to things as they happen, accept them for what they are, and let them go when they pass.

No Self—Every individual's identity is also constantly changing and in transition. Our minds and bodies are an amazing collection of cells and energy in perpetual motion. The person we were yesterday, or even one hour, one minute, or one second ago is already different from the person we are right now.

The Source of Suffering—To fail to realize that the first two marks of existence are true will cause unhappiness and dissatisfaction because we will continue to want the world to be other than what it is.

Volumes of books have been written on each of these *three marks of existence*, but if we consider them in a very straightforward, simple way, they're easy to grasp. The hardest one to swallow is the second, because we like to think that we have control over who we are, and that the person each of us thinks of as "me" is a solid, constant, reliable being. But all you have to do is consider who you were ten years ago and it becomes obvious that your views, memories, emotions, and thoughts are constantly in flux. The bright side is that because our thoughts, feelings, and bodies are always changing, we are constantly becoming someone new, and, potentially, someone better.

So basically, the first step to leading a more blissful life is a big one, but not a hard one. All we need is a willingness to acknowledge what our expectations are, gently put them aside, and attempt to comprehend the nature of impermanence.

Step 2: *Right Intentions*

If you're interested in Buddhism, it's probably because you want to live a more content life—and give other people as much happiness and as little grief as possible. That humanitarian outlook is what

Step #2 is all about—approaching Buddhism, and life in general, with the desire to overcome our own suffering and prevent the suffering of others. For those of us who aren't trying to become monks (Buddha referred to us as "householders"), that doesn't mean rejecting capitalist society, never planning for the future, or giving away all of our money and possessions to the poor. But it does mean having a genuinely kind, open-minded outlook as often as we can swing it.

Some books about Buddhism call this step *right thought* because Buddha taught that thoughts are the origin of all intentions. In his words:

> *Mind is the forerunner of all things. If you act based on kindness and wisdom in the mind, happiness will follow you like the wheel of a chariot follows the ox which draws it. And if you act based on unkindness or you act from an unwise state of mind, then unhappiness follows just as the wheel of the cart follows the ox which draws it.*

I definitely don't have a mind full of kindness and wisdom. The closest I've come to achieving this goal is to recognize when I'm thinking crappy thoughts and try to hose them down before they turn into words or actions—sometimes I'm successful, sometimes I'm not. Even great Buddhist teachers still feel anger and have less than saintly inclinations, but they've gotten better at handling those negative emotions and urges. They've learned to put space between the emotion or urge and their actions, space that allows them to react carefully and skillfully to the situation (for the most part, it's meditation that helps them get better at this). As beginners, if we can label a negative emotion, thought, or urge as just that—negative, unhelpful, highly likely to make things worse—we're already on the path to having the *right intentions*.

Step 3: *Right Speech*

The third step is to examine our impact on the world, starting with what we say. This is a rough one for me. Speaking before thinking has always been my basic MO. In the past I've defended this habit as my being bold, direct, and willing to tell it as it is. But in most cases, my doing so has ended up making someone miserable—usually me. Before opening our mouths, Buddha suggests that we ask ourselves if what we're about to say is: 1) what we truly think or feel and 2) likely to have a positive or negative effect on the situation. If we have an honest opinion that is likely to hurt someone, we should ask ourselves if it's really necessary to share that opinion. Will it help the situation? If not, let it go unsaid. And that applies to talking about ourselves, too.

I imagine that a Buddhist monk has a much easier time doing this than you or I. Monks don't go to cocktail parties or on dates, when a gap in the conversation feels painfully awkward. They don't get into arguments with significant others during which they become hurt or confused, and struggle desperately while trying to explain themselves. They aren't bombarded with manipulative media—photos in magazines, images on television, ads everywhere—that are just begging for critical commentary. And they aren't surrounded by friends who consider making fun of strangers an enjoyable social pastime. We, on the other hand, have to deal with all of those factors and more. So keeping unnecessary negativity out of the conversation takes a lot of determination. Thankfully, the countless benefits of speaking positively—that is, like a generally optimistic, nonjudgmental person, not a maniacally upbeat member of a folk dancing troupe—become obvious pretty quickly. Life feels more fun. Other people enjoy hanging out with you more. Even though you continue to notice the bad stuff, you dwell on it less.

Step 4: *Right Action*

Naturally, after speech comes action. We all have our own ideas about what is considered ethical and what isn't. And chances are, our ideas are right most of the time. So this is Buddha saying that we should always try to act in accordance with our ethics. If we get a nagging feeling that what we're about to do isn't right, then we shouldn't do it. In most cases, it requires more energy and effort to behave ethically than it does to just let our ethics slide. But it pays spiritually to muster that energy. At the end of the day, we feel happier about who we are.

That said, doing the "right thing" is often complicated and confusing. Because it's impossible to know what all the various results of our actions will be one second, ten minutes, a year, or a decade from now, all we can do is act carefully, intelligently, and with the best intentions. It's like voting for president when you disagree with each of the candidates on a few of the issues. Or having to choose between hitting a rabbit on the highway or swerving out of the way and possibly causing an accident. Sometimes we do "the right thing" to different degrees, depending on how much of our own comfort we're willing to sacrifice. A friend once told me about a day when an old man collapsed in pain right in front of him. The man was homeless, covered in grime, and reeked of his own urine and feces. My friend called 911 and then stayed by the man's side until the ambulance came. He knew it would be kinder to try and comfort the man, to hold his head or at least his hand, but the guy smelled so bad he didn't want to touch him, so he just stood a few feet away and waited. His attempt to live by his ethics— to help people in need whenever possible—wasn't perfect, but it was pretty good. The only sane option is to do what we can handle, when we can handle it.

Buddha believed that there exist some very basic ways to act right. When a large group of male and female students began to flock to him after his enlightenment, they asked for some rules to follow in their desire to refrain from harming themselves and others. He gave them these five precepts for getting along:

1. Do not speak dishonestly.
2. Do not take what isn't given to or meant for you.
3. Do not kill other living things or ask that they be killed for you.
4. Do not engage in sexual activity that might harm you or others.
5. Do not become intoxicated to the point where you can't control your speech or actions.

Pretty standard, commonsense stuff. But hardly easy to live by. As with every other philosophy in this book, the underlying promise is that choosing to accept and act in accordance with it will actually lead to your greater happiness and satisfaction. Living by it is actually a very unselfish way to be self-serving.

The Bold and the Buddhaful

"I remember when I was just starting to practice meditation—twenty-four years old, trying to come to grips with my life. I was holed up in my shitty little apartment for months at a time, just doing tai chi and doing my best to do sitting practice. I had a very clear feeling that I'd always been in meditation, that I'd never left meditation. That it was a much more substantial reality than what we normally take to be reality. That was very clear to me even then, but it's taken me this long in my life to bring it out into the world more, through more time practicing, watching my mind, trying to generate *bodhicitta* [loving-kindness]."—Richard Gere

"I don't know whether I believe in God or not. I think, really, I'm some kind of Buddhist."   —Henri Matisse

"Buddhism is kind of the underpinning to all I do; it's understanding that you are not your little problems, that everything is flux."   —Duncan Sheik

"My father, when very young, was the first American to be ordained as a Buddhist monk. He now teaches Indo-Tibetan studies at Columbia University and is regarded as this country's foremost authority on Buddhism. When the Dalai Lama comes to America, it's my father who is his host. When asked if

I consider myself Buddhist, the answer is, 'Not really.' But it's more my religion than any other because I was brought up with it in an intellectual and spiritual environment. I don't practice or preach it, however. But Buddhism has had a major effect on who I am and how I think about the world."

—Uma Thurman

"I grew up with kids whose parents were in the industry, and after a while I realized that material wealth didn't lead to happiness. So at one point I found a book on Buddhism. And then I went to Columbia University and I took a course given by Robert Thurman who is the world's pre-eminent thinker in Indo-Buddhism—he's actually Uma's father. I took every class he taught and it's just sort of infiltrated my life so that everywhere I go, I try to keep some perspective because I know this town can be illusory and can lead you in wrong directions."

—Jake Gyllenhaal

"[Buddhist chanting] is something that one depends on like—I think, like, I need my refrigerator, I need the clothing on my back, I need shelter. And chanting takes care of that spiritual side, that subconscious mind that I tap into."   —Tina Turner

STEP 5: *Engage in Right Livelihood*

Our "livelihood" refers to our jobs. And *right livelihood* in the Buddhist sense means not knowingly having a job that causes harm to living things. Like *right action,* the reality of *right livelihood* is that we should simply try to come as close as possible to attaining the ideal at any given time in our lives. It's very difficult to find a job that doesn't involve wasting resources or polluting the environment. Sometimes we have the opportunity to choose who we work for and in what capacity. Sometimes we don't. As a journalist who often writes for magazines, I feel conflicted about the messages some of them send to readers about what their bodies should look like and what their values should be. On certain days I feel sure that I'm writing materialistic propaganda that's encouraging people to live beyond their means, spiral into crippling debt, and ruin their lives. On other days I'm confident that my articles are providing people with important information and inspiring them to live the lives they want. The truth is that like most other commercial endeavors, magazines have their good and bad points.

Every job will probably involve making some compromises; the question to ask ourselves is how much we're compromising our ideals, and whether we feel comfortable with that amount. Do you generally feel good about what you do? If the answer is yes, then you can still make small changes that will make you feel even better. If the answer is no, it may be time for a major change. (But more about that in Chapter Four).

Believe nothing, no matter where you read it, or who said it, no matter if I have said it, unless it agrees with your own reason and your own common sense.

Step 6: *True Effort*

Everyone who decides to formally become a Buddhist is choosing to dedicate most of their time and energy to following the guidelines of *the eightfold path*—to give their *true effort* to realizing nirvana. Each part of the path is connected and a necessary step to fulfilling the others. A person who practices *right speech* and *right action* isn't likely to have a problem developing *right mindfulness* and *right contemplation* (below). Though all eight steps are unique and essential, they're pretty much variations on a single theme of living a Buddhist, or "awake" life. For those of us who want to benefit from Buddhism without devoting ourselves to it in a more formal way, *true effort* applies more to putting our hearts into everything that we do—whether it's picking out groceries, listening to someone talk, or taking a yoga class. While we're there and doing it, we should be there and nowhere else. We should try to be present in the moment. *True effort* is also a reminder to try and face every new moment with energy and vitality—because keeping our minds front and center can be hard work.

If we consider *the eightfold path* a list of ideals to value highly and do our best to realize when and how we can, we can't go wrong.

Step 7: *Right Mindfulness*

It's impossible to overemphasize how central paying close attention to what we think and what we do is to the practice of Buddhism. Buddha taught that the reason we're so often unhappy is because we don't see things as they really are. We're too caught up in our own perceptions, too distracted by our memories of the past and our hopes for and expectations of the future, as well as by endlessly guessing at what other people in our lives are thinking and doing. All of this makes it impossible for us to just BE. And that's not even accounting for the distractions that come from outside our own heads—TV, gossip, music, books, games, movies, etc. Our minds have the ability to work like blenders and, without realizing it, we constantly hold down the button marked "puree"—causing our thoughts and impressions to spin out of control at such a high speed that they become wildly mixed up and distorted. That's why when you're sitting there mulling over your life as well as what's going on in the rest of the world and someone asks you what you're thinking about, you can't come up with a single thing. There is no single thing—there are dozens of them, all struggling for your attention like a room full of four-year-olds. Or sometimes there are just a few thoughts or worries repeating themselves over and over and over and over. Arghhhh!

Mindfulness—being aware of our thoughts, our words, our actions—is very difficult to maintain some of the time, much less all of the time. That's where meditation comes in. Meditation is mindfulness training. People usually sit still or walk very slowly when they meditate because it's so difficult to actually focus on everything your body is doing. While they consciously sit or walk, they pay careful attention to the thoughts whizzing around in their minds and then they slow those thoughts down, separate them, and eventually tame them so that they stop getting in the way of basic, everyday happiness. Through his studies and experiences, Buddha discovered that mindfulness was crucial to happiness, and that meditation was the best way to learn to become mindful. But for starters, the idea is to simply pay attention to what's going on around us right here, right now—to focus all five of our senses front and center.

STEP 8: *Right Contemplation*

This step is about staying focused and thinking deeply. While a major goal of Buddhism is to develop the ability to stay connected to the present moment, so is intelligently pondering the big picture. This eighth step of the path is called *right contemplation* because it involves contemplating different aspects of life—the past, the present, the future, your community, the world, art, music, the sciences, etc.—at different times, as is appropriate and helpful. It's wise to give careful, focused thought to what it is we want for the world, for ourselves, and for the people we love. It's also wise to give careful, focused thought to how our words and actions might affect ourselves and others down the line (we can't actually know what will happen but we can make an effort to ensure that we don't knowingly hurt ourselves or anyone else). Contrary to what most people think, the lifestyle of a non-monastic Buddhist isn't isolated or passive. Remember, the word "Buddha" means "awakened one." An awake person is very aware and that awareness leads to intelligent, productive actions.

Another aspect of *right contemplation* is the ability to view the world in both practical and "absolute" terms. In absolute terms, a Buddhist looks at the world and sees that nothing in it—not a person or a thing or a feeling—is solid or definite. For example, a chair isn't just a chair. It is lumber and paint and glue; it is a tree; it is water and air and earth; it is molecules and empty space; in a different situation it's firewood; it may be used as a table or a footstool; it may be taken apart and made into something else entirely. The chair it was five seconds ago is not the chair it is now because of the millions of minute changes happening to it that we can't even see. A person who has never seen a chair before might mistake it for something else. The chair itself might be a figment of our imagination, or maybe the chair actually is something else and we've mistaken it for a chair. Do you feel like you're back in Philosophy 101? Like any good philosopher, a Buddhist recognizes the boundaries and order that human beings have imposed on nature for the sake of convenience, safety, productivity, pleasure, etc.—and they can see through those fabrications to the more mysterious, boundless truth beyond it.

But in practical terms a chair is just a chair. When Buddhists walk into a room, they know what to sit on. *Right contemplation* suggests that we always keep in mind the simultaneous mysteries and practicalities of life. Like the chair, we are always changing and can be perceived hundreds of different ways. You might be a sister to one person, a friend to another, a girlfriend to someone else. You might be a mentor to someone younger than you, and a protégée to someone older. If you live in your hometown, you're a local. If you're on vacation in another country, you're a foreigner. You might be a completely different person when you're sad or angry than who you are when you're in a good mood. Some days you might remember one set of events and stories, and another day you might have forgotten them. And yet, in the practical sense, when someone calls and asks for you, it's always you who picks up the phone. It's very simple and pretty mind-blowing at the same time. But that's Buddhism for you.

· · · · · · ·

Meditation Starter Kit

Why Meditate? Buddhist philosophy is full of common sense theories and advice that is easy to agree with, but not so easy to put into practice. Even when we know that we should curb our expectations, stay focused on the present, and be honest about the way the world really is, it's difficult to do so when our minds are spinning out of control—analyzing the past, planning for the future, and just wandering all over the place in the present. Meditation is the only way that Buddha found to completely quiet his mind and stop letting his thoughts and emotions get the best of him. Because, as meditation will make obvious to you very quickly, you are neither your thoughts nor your emotions. They merely happen *to* you.

Location: Find an uncluttered, quiet spot indoors or outdoors.

Supplies: Wear comfortable clothes and grab two pillows off of your bed, plus a blanket, thick beach towel, or yoga mat (check out what made-for-meditation cushions look like on www.zafu.net).

Prep: Make sure phones, stereo, TV, pager, etc. are turned off. Put all nonmeditating pets and/or significant others in another room.

How to Sit: You don't actually have to sit on the floor to meditate. But the point of sitting a very particular way every time you meditate is to let both your body and your mind know that what you're about to do is different from all the other things you do all day. Eventually you start to equate sitting in just that way with meditating, which helps you to stay focused. There's also something motivating about knowing that everyone else who does sitting meditation assumes a similar position. So fold your beach towel or yoga mat in half (or fold your blanket so that it's about three feet square) and then kneel on top of it with your legs about shoulder width apart. Now fold one pillow in half, place it behind your knees and sit on it. Does that feel comfortable? If not, try folding the second pillow and stacking it on top of the first to lift your butt up a little higher. How's that? If you'd prefer, you can sit your butt on the pillow and cross your legs in front of you (raising your tush takes some pressure off of your folded legs). Once your lower body is settled, straighten your back, rest your forearms on your thighs, and let your hands relax in your lap. To keep them together without tension, rest one hand inside the other and cross your thumbs. Now fix and hold your gaze at a spot about a foot in front of you on the floor (or grass or sand or wherever you happen to be sitting), or on a blank spot on the wall in front of you, about a foot up from the ground. Your eyes should remain aimed at the spot, but still relaxed—look, but don't stare. Your head should be tilted slightly downward. To help maintain good posture, imagine that there is a string tied to the crown of your head, pulling you up. Roll your shoulders gently back (no slouching). OK, you're ready.

How Not to Think: There are many different methods of meditating, but I've found that the best beginning meditation consists of simply learning how to let go of thoughts instead of getting carried away by them. Start your meditation by just relaxing. Give yourself credit for doing this in the first place. Then bring yourself into your body: How does the pillow feel under your butt? It is hot or cold in the room? Are there noises in the distance? What can you smell? Make a mental note of it all. OK, now leave those thoughts behind and try to clear your mind for a second. Consider Buddhist master Sogyal Rinpoche's advice on meditation (from www.buddhanet

.net): "You just quietly sit, your body still, your speech silent, your mind at ease, and allow thoughts to come and go, without letting them play havoc on you." Imagine that your mind is a cool, dark pond and that your thoughts are goldfish. When a thought pops into your head, imagine that it's a fish jumping out of the surface of the pond. See the thought, but don't try to catch it. Just let it dive back down into the dark water and disappear. In less than a second, another thought will jump out of the water—or maybe two or three thoughts at the same time. Just let them dive back down again. At first, you can expect countless fish/ thoughts flying through the air. Try not to get frustrated. Every once in a while you'll accidentally hook onto a thought and your mind will get reeled in. Before you know it, you've been thinking for ten minutes straight. That's OK. As soon as you realize what's happening, picture the dark, smooth-as-glass surface of the pond again. Sometimes it helps to say the word "thinking" when a thought pops up. By labeling a thought as simply a thought, you're able to create some distance between yourself and your thoughts. You start to realize that your thoughts and "you" are two different things, which is the very beginning of discovering a deeper, more real you.

You're Meditating!

Tip: Try not to judge your thoughts as smart, stupid, funny, selfish, horny, or anything else. Just label them "thoughts" and let them fade away.

Tip: Be prepared, because you're about to discover some nutty things about how your mind works. You might think a lot of the same thoughts repeatedly. You might suddenly realize solutions to problems you've been mulling over for weeks. You might discover that you can't stop thinking about how cute Jake Gyllenhaal is in spite of his annoying doe-eyed look. No matter how much fun you're having listening to yourself think, do your best to keep clearing your mind again and again.

Tip: Don't expect much—or even any—mental silence at first. Our brains are pretty hell-bent on keeping the ideas coming. Be patient with yourself.

Tip: Keep your first few forays into meditating short and sweet to help ensure that you'll do it again. Five or ten minutes is plenty. You can do it for longer when and if you feel like it.

~ Meditation Menu ~

In his book *How to Practice*, His Holiness the Dalai Lama presents a few different ways to meditate in order to achieve the state of mind that he calls *calm abiding*, or relaxed awareness. He suggests doing the one you prefer (or you can alternate between different styles) for five minutes a few times a day.

MEDITATE ON THE BREATH

What it does: Breathing meditation is a little like mental boot camp. It may seem overly simple, but its purpose is to train, sharpen, and strengthen the mind so it becomes a tool we can use, rather than something that is constantly getting the best of us. During some Buddhist retreats, breathing meditation is practiced for two or three days before moving on to other types of meditation.

How to do it: Focus only on the sensation of air coming in and out through your nose (or, alternately, you can focus on the rising and falling of your abdomen as you breathe). Try not to think of anything other than the air flowing through your body. As soon as you notice that your mind has wandered, gently return your focus to the air passing in and out of your nose.

MEDITATE ON IMPERMANENCE

What it does: Meditating on the impermanent nature of the world helps us to stop expecting good things to last or bad things never to happen and to accept that everything is always coming and going. Reminding ourselves that all things are always in flux makes us better able to deal with life's ups and downs. Meditating on impermanence also helps us to carefully choose which thoughts and feelings merit action, and which should simply be allowed to pass on by.

How to do it: Sit quietly and try to identify each new thought, image, or sensation as it enters your mind. Label each thought "thinking," each sensation "feeling," and each image "imagining," then try to let go of it rather than get involved with it. You'll soon notice that one thought quickly replaces another. Your body is constantly bombarding you with sensations, and your imagination is basically running wild. Even if your head feels like a jungle, keep trying to separate and label each thought, feeling, and image and then let it go.

MEDITATE ON YOUR ACTIONS

What it does: Paying careful attention to our movements helps us both to stay in the present moment and to act wisely and skillfully rather than thoughtlessly and clumsily.

How to do it: Instead of just doing things without thinking, try to acknowledge every little thing that you're doing. As this is no easy task, stick to simple actions such as walking, doing the dishes, or brushing your teeth. Focus on exactly how you're moving your body. Feel the pressure of your body against the objects you're touching and the pressure they exert back. You don't have to assign words to what you're feeling; just be aware of each and every action and your corresponding feelings.

MEDITATE ON AN IMAGE

What it does: Like breathing meditation, meditating on an image helps train your mind to stay sharp and focused.

How to do it: Choose an image and place it at eye level about four feet in front of you. A small statue of Buddha is always a nice thing to meditate on, as it reminds you of your lofty goals, but the image can really be of anything. A picture of Russell

Crowe would do just as well. Stare at the image for a few minutes and then close your eyes and try to reproduce it in your mind. This is harder than it sounds. The image will keep slipping away and you'll have difficulty remembering certain details. Every time the image begins to waver, renew your effort and put it back together again. If you need to, open your eyes and look at the image to refresh your memory. Try not to "think" about things that you associate with the image. Try to see it as something separate from any attachments. Every time your mind begins to tell a story about the image, put on the brakes and come back to simply seeing the image.

2

The Tao of
Taking Things in Stride

My last boyfriend, let's call him Dave, was as unflappable as Gandhi. It drove me nuts. One Saturday morning, only a few hours past the crack of dawn, we were standing in a mile-long line waiting to buy tickets to the U.S. Open tennis tournament. Now, I like tennis, but Dave *loves* tennis. And this was a day when Venus and Serena were scheduled to play each other on center court. We'd already been shivering in the same spot for forty-five minutes when a security guard walked over and tried to reorganize the line. He instantly created chaos and a group of people used the opportunity to sneak further toward the front. After a blur of khaki and pastel, Dave and I found ourselves a good twenty places behind where we had been before. Naturally, I was annoyed. So I started to complain—about the clueless security guard, the jerks who cut the line, and what a hassle it was to get tickets to this uppity sport that requires powerful female athletes to don pleated miniskirts and little white briefs. My mood was circling the drain. It wasn't that I minded waiting longer for tickets—I didn't even care if I got in—I was just miffed by the stupidity of it all. I looked over at Dave, who I expected would be even more frustrated than I since this event meant so much to him. But as usual, he was a poster-boy for patience and tolerance. And, as usual, that pissed me off even more. When I asked how it was that he wasn't peeved, he said "Getting mad isn't going to make things any better." Which is pretty much the most aggravating thing you can say to a person who is already mad. It's like telling Mike Tyson to "Relax." He was lucky I didn't punch him.

People like Dave seem to have been born with the ability to let things roll off their back. The rest of us have to train ourselves to take things in stride. To that end, Buddha suggested a very simple practice of allowing emotions to come and go without holding on to them and letting them take us for a ride. Developing this skill can mean the difference between fighting and talking, crying and giggling, making things worse and making them better. It enables us to stay more positive and lighthearted in the face of negative, suffocating emotions. This little trick—which gets easier and easier every time you try it—is an incredibly effective means for loosening the emotions that tend to put us into a headlock the minute we feel them: anger, jealousy, disappointment, insult, abandonment, betrayal, rejection, disrespect, or just annoyance. Whether our usual response to any of these hellish emotions is to lash out (complain, insult, blame, ridicule), shut down (clam up, leave, deny), or collapse (cry, get depressed), it's usually a knee-jerk reaction that seems completely uncontrollable. Something frustrating or annoying or hurtful happens, and the next thing we know, we're doing what we always do—and it isn't pretty.

In order to break old patterns of behavior, it helps to understand one of the fundamental theories of Buddhism, which is that thoughts and feelings, and our reactions to them, are not a solid or fixed part of who we are. They are as separate from our identity as fish are separate from the water they swim in. Ideas and emotions pass through our minds and bodies the way that clouds pass through the sky. At least some of them do. There are others that we desperately hold on to and have a hard time letting go of. The ironic thing is that the ones we cling to the most are usually the most unpleasant. When we feel or think something painful, there's a tendency to continue thinking and feeling it. Not because we want to, but because we can't stop. We obsess. We can't get over that awful thing that happened, that horrible mistake that we made, that fear or insecurity that feels like an arrow in our side. That's why meditating is so important. Sitting quietly and observing how our mind works makes it obvious that the intrinsic nature of thoughts and feelings is to pop up and fade away, pop up and fade away. We don't have to let one feeling or thought stick in our mind and drive us crazy. With practice, we can develop the ability to let it pass. Or, if not pass, at least stop it from taking us over.

The Hole in the Doughnut

The Buddhist view that *everything* is constantly changing, and that nothing is permanent, makes the question of identity a complicated one. Because the contents of your mind and the physical sensations in your body are continually in flux, they aren't who you are. Your body, although you may always smile the same way, walk with the same gait, have the same voice, etc., is also not who you are. You are not your arm. You are not your leg. You are not your voice. You're not even your head, even though that's where all the action goes down. Your personality, the part of you that seems to be there every morning when you get up—the part that thinks Ben Stiller is funny but never laughs at Jay Leno, the part that has always preferred white sheets to colored ones, the part that cries at sappy AT&T commercials when you're PMSing, the part that remembers hating high school gym class—as permanent as it might feel, also changes. Our tastes change, our perspective on certain memories changes, even our sense of humor changes.

But through everything, Buddhists *do* believe that there is a being who is experiencing all that change, who is connected to all that knowledge, who grasps at certain ideas and rejects others, who can step back during meditation and see it all happening, and *that* being is who you are. You are there at the center of it all, but you are separate from it all. That's not to say that you don't have a personality that other people recognize each time they see you. Of course you do. Everybody does. But you are also separate from your personality. One of the most amazing benefits of meditation is discovering the true nature of identity. One Buddhist teacher described identity as the hole in the doughnut. You're empty of any permanent, unchangeable characteristics, but you're still there in the middle, hanging out.

You know how you wake up the morning after a big fight with someone you love, and suddenly all the anger and frustration you were feeling the night before has dissipated like a fog? You realize how pointless it all was, how unimportant in the grand scheme of things, how much better it would have been if you'd just taken it all in stride instead of lashing out, shutting down, or collapsing. Now, after it's all over, you feel open and emotionally soft. You're ready to talk instead of argue. You struggle to understand exactly what happened, to remember what was said. What did it all mean? This is you seeking clarity and wisdom about twelve hours too late. What we really need to do is achieve that wisdom and clarity— and that ability to let things pass—when we can really use it: at that very moment when the shit hits the fan.

TURN ANGER INTO AIR

When a sticky situation comes up, we become almost instantly flooded with emotions like annoyance, frustration, anger, sadness, or fear. Those emotions feel solid and suffocating—they fill us up like concrete and start to harden fast, so that we feel trapped and helpless. How can we not give in to anger or sadness or jealousy when it's filling us from head to toe? A simple version of a Buddhist practice called *tonglen* can help prevent unpleasant situations from getting us down and triggering negative reactions that make everything worse.

Tonglen is the practice of acting like a human filter: breathing in bad emotions and thoughts, filtering out the negative stuff, and exhaling only good (or at least neutral) things. Instead of letting negativity get the best of us or relying on someone else to make the situation better, *tonglen* allows us to take on the responsibility ourselves by using our own bodies and minds. Every human being is capable of doing this, no matter how cynical, skeptical, or cranky she may be on the surface. At our core, we are all fundamentally good, fundamentally compassionate, and fundamentally kind. Every Buddhist believes this to be true—that deep down we all would prefer ourselves and the people around us to be happy. By tapping into that core goodness and filtering negative emotions through it, it becomes much more difficult to act like a jerk or collapse into sadness. As we practice *tonglen* again and again, it has a stronger and more positive effect on us and whomever or whatever we're grappling with.

"The Buddhist way is first to distance ourselves from what's causing us trouble. If we can't distance ourselves physically, we can do so mentally. This gives space in which to study the cause of our distress."

—*Venerable Adrienne Howley, author of* The Naked Buddha

Here's how it goes: Let's say you're at dinner with your family and your mother says something that you find insensitive and critical—like the time mine called me a spinster because I was twenty-nine years old and still single. Your muscles instantly tense up. Your body temperature rises. You stop breathing for a second. One of your buttons has been pushed and it's sending your internal systems into turmoil. That concrete is hardening up fast and you are about to spit something back . . . Now, right now, is when you have to do something radically different.

1. Open up. You know how things have usually gone in the past. Now you have to open up to the idea that they can go differently. Take a few seconds to create space for change. Push memories of other encounters like this one out of your head and imagine a large, white, empty room where you can start fresh. In this room there is no past, nothing is predictable, anything is possible.

2. Inhale the bad. Imagine that the unpleasant thoughts and feelings that you're experiencing are a big cloud of smoke. Visualize that smoke clouding up around you. Now breathe it in. Breathe it deep into your abdomen. Let your stomach become soft and full of it. Take a second to accept the fact that sadness, frustration, anger, and disappointment are all commonplace, everyday emotions that come and go all the time. Now imagine that every time you breathe in, some of that smoke dissolves and all that's left is cool, clean air. You're not absorbing the smoke or holding it in. Despite the fact that we have spent our entire lives making a habit of holding onto them, emotions and thoughts have no substance. If we release our hold on them, they cease to exist. Imagine them entering your body with each breath and then fading into nothing.

3. Exhale the good. When you exhale, imagine breathing out cool, fresh air into the situation. Now breathe in and filter more. Keep breathing and filtering, transforming crappy feelings into calm, breezy ones. This will feel completely pointless at first. It won't seem to help at all. But if you hang in there and keep at it, it will start to change how you feel. For me, it helps to repeat a mantra as I breathe, something like "breathe in hurt, breathe out kindness," or "breathe in anger, breathe out for-giveness." It also helps to keep your neck, shoulders, jaw, and stomach soft instead of tense. Refuse to let the negative feel-ings get stuck inside of you. Somewhere in the course of every breath, allow them to lose their heat and heaviness, to thin out until they disappear. All that is left is coolness and light.

I'll be the first to admit that *tonglen* is tough to do those first few times when you're really upset. That's why it's a good idea to prac-tice it on a regular basis, so that it will come to you more easily in those crucial moments. Many Buddhists will sit on their meditation cushions and practice *tonglen* for a few minutes every day, so that it feels like second nature. Broadening their scope beyond their own personal lives, they imagine breathing in the frustration, anger, and sadness of the entire world and letting it dissolve inside of them. Pema Chödrön, a Buddhist nun, author, and teacher, gives a very in-depth explanation of *tonglen* meditation in her excellent book *Start Where You Are*. But the basic version of *tonglen* above can be help-ful all by itself, whenever we choose to use it. It gives us a chance to disarm our own and other people's negative emotions, instead of just reacting in the same old unproductive way.

· · · · · · ·

Mini-Meditation Trick: Stop Obsessing!

Our minds' ability to keep harping on one fear or worry is an enormous drag. A single idea can go around and around in our brains and we CAN'T STOP THINKING ABOUT IT. The Dalai Lama's advice in cases like this is to try the standard meditation technique of focusing just on your breath. Feel it coming in and going out of your body, and try to think of nothing but each breath. But he is also wise enough to know that some of our anxieties are so loud and persistent that breathing isn't enough to distract our brains. So when breathing doesn't work, he suggests a very specific chant. The basic Buddhist meditation chant is om mani padme hum *(pronounced "om mani padmay hum"—there is no literal translation because it is a sacred, symbolic sound that represents all of the teachings of Buddha at once). Chant these sounds over and over again in a steady rhythm. Feel the vibrations they make in your throat, chest, and stomach. Set an egg timer and give yourself at least one full minute to get on a chanting roll. After that you may not want to stop for a while. Chanting provides a blessed break from endless obsessing. It works best out loud, but chanting silently to yourself will do in a pinch, so don't hesitate to repeat* om mani padme hum *anytime, anywhere.*

BEWARE: YOUR GUTS MIGHT BE FULL OF IT

Besides avoiding making a bad situation worse, another very good reason not to lash out, break down, or withdraw at the moment when we're most upset is that our gut reactions are often dishonest. We think that by reacting immediately, we're expressing how we sincerely feel, but a little examination might reveal that it's all just smoke and mirrors—a front for deeper feelings that we haven't come to terms with yet. Take, for example, a scene that happened later that same afternoon I was at the U.S. Open. Not one of my better days. I had never met one of Dave's female friends before and was freaked out to discover that she was very flirtatious and physically affectionate with him. She would frequently grab onto his arm as they were talking and when she laughed she would collapse against him, holding on to him for support. About halfway through the tournament, she decided to show us all her new tattoo—

a snake slinking its way down her lower back (presumably on its way into her butt crack)—by yanking down her jeans and bending over directly in front of Dave. That was too much for me, and I asked her if she actually enjoyed shoving live animals up her ass or if the tattoo was just symbolic. Our interactions deteriorated from there. When Dave asked what my problem was, I said I didn't like his friend because she was obnoxious, desperate for attention, and clearly throwing herself at him. I think I called her a bimbo. And that's the position I held for a long time.

After beginning to meditate and examine my own motivations, I soon realized that the real reasons I didn't like snake-girl were different from the story I told Dave. The truth was that I wanted to be the only woman who could command his attention like that. I was afraid of losing him, afraid that he might find her more attractive, fun, and wild than me. Afraid that I constantly had to compete with other women for the number one spot in his heart. Had I met her on my own at a party or through work, I probably would have enjoyed her nuttiness and thought her tattoo was over-the-top but commendably ballsy. Without Dave around, I could've really liked this chick. But my own competitiveness and fear made me want to cut her down. It also made me angry at Dave for choosing the kind of female friend who seemed threatening to me. Writing her off as a bimbo and drama queen was a way for me to ignore my true emotions—good old fear and insecurity. It doesn't take much soul-searching to find out that they are behind most of the behavior that makes people unhappy. What was new to me was that awareness— the core of Buddhist practice—is all it takes to make us able to see and react to the truth more clearly.

Taking the time to find out the truth about what's really bothering us gives us a chance to dig out problems by the roots. There are many different types of meditation. While some forms are meant to help us discover the true nature of the mind and so require us to acknowledge and then let go of all feelings and thoughts as soon as they arise, meditation can sometimes be used as a tool for reflection and examination. Let's say that you're in a relationship and are having all sorts of confusing feelings about your significant other. When you think about him, you get a big lump in your chest and it feels very overwhelming. By sitting down in meditation position and focusing on that ball of emotion you can slowly peel it like an onion and find out what's really going on in there. It's a lot like psychoanalyzing yourself. Continually try to delve deeper into why you act and feel the way you do. Don't try to understand why the other person acts or feels a certain way, because it's beyond your ability to know. Just focus on yourself and keep asking the question *why*. It's shocking how quickly you'll start learning new things about yourself. And if they're unflattering things, you will no doubt want to stop meditating immediately and go have a beer. But it's only by staying there and facing the truth that you'll be able to make changes for the better. When you get down to the nitty-gritty of what's going on—and you'll know when that happens—that's the right time to sit down with your guy and let it all out.

Monks Gone Wild: Snowbound

 In 1976, Tenzin Palmo, a British-born Tibetan Buddhist, was living in a monastery in India where women were considered intellectually and spiritually inferior to men. When the thirty-three-year-old nun complained to her teacher that the sexism felt like a major obstacle on her path to enlightenment, he advised that she meditate in solitude. That sounded like a good idea to Tenzin, so she found a small cave high in the snowy Himalayas and happily stayed there for the next *twelve years*. She meditated for four hours, three times a day, while perched in a raised wooden box that kept her body off of the wet ground. She slept sitting up in the box every night. When not meditating, she melted snow to drink and grew turnips and potatoes. While there she repeated ten million mantras, which itself took three years. Her goal was to let go of all desires and become fully accepting of the nature of imper-

manence. She told a newspaper reporter at the *Toronto Star* that she never felt lonely and only stayed so long because she enjoyed it so much. "I really loved it," she said. "I felt relaxed and spacious and inwardly fulfilled." Since leaving her cave (which she was forced to do when an Indian immigration officer tracked her down to inform her that her visa had expired), Tenzin has started a Buddhist monastery for women. You can check on her progress at www.tenzinpalmo.com.

CURB YOUR EXPECTATIONS

To experience more bliss in life, there's one habit we *must* break: constantly forming expectations about what the future will hold. Though we seldom realize it, our expectations chip away at our overall happiness bit by bit. Last year my boyfriend and I went to Las Vegas solely because I had been offered a free "luxury" hotel room by a public relations agent with whom I had done business in the past. I imagined that the room would be cheesy, but *fun* cheesy— a suite with a heart-shaped hot tub, a king-sized vibrating bed, a terrace with French doors, champagne, and chocolate-covered strawberries. When we got there, it turned out to be a Howard Johnson's–style room circa 1970 with cigarette-burned bedspreads, a TV chained to the wall, and a mustard-yellow bathroom with water stains on the ceiling. Had I not been expecting Clark Kent and Lois Lane's Niagara Falls honeymoon suite I would have probably reveled in the old-school, authentic Vegas vibe and ordered a whiskey sour from room service. But I was so disappointed—and pissed off at that PR agent for giving me the wrong impression— that I wanted to cry. I was crushed, and embarrassed that I had bragged to my boyfriend about how glitzy it was going to be. That room, which we stayed in for only one night before finding a better one, cast a gloom over the trip that never really lifted. I knew at the time that it was stupid to let such an insignificant thing get me down, but I had been so attached to my ideas of what it was going to be like that I couldn't shake my disappointment.

The weird thing is that we don't just get disappointed when we think something is going to be amazing and it turns out crummy. Often our hearts sink just because something turns out *differently* from what we expected. We don't give reality a chance to make us happy because we're too preoccupied with our preconceived ideas. Buddha taught that in order to avoid unhappiness, we must learn to curb our expectations and stay open to whatever life offers. This doesn't mean we shouldn't hope for things—hope we get a raise, hope the guy we're flirting with will flirt back, hope it doesn't rain during our vacation. But there's a difference between hoping and becoming fixated on a particular outcome to the point where you feel that if it doesn't happen the way you imagined it, the world is ending. That's what we need to avoid. How? By practicing the art of being unassuming and flexible, and accepting the way things are.

It will come as no surprise that Buddha discovered that the best way to get used to remaining open to and accepting of the present, whatever it might consist of, is through meditation. Meditation trains our minds to stay in the moment, and not to give in to the urge to fantasize about the future. But even if we don't meditate on a daily or weekly basis, we can still practice catching ourselves falling into fantasy mode. Whenever you "wake up" in the middle of a daydream in which you're imagining how a certain event will go, what a specific place will be like, or how a person will behave, mentally put on the brakes and remind yourself that life is unpredictable, that anything can happen, that fantasizing can easily lead to disappointment. Then imagine reeling your mind back from the future and into the present. Feel yourself breathing, pay attention to what's in front of you, to the noises coming into your ears and the smells coming in through your nose. What is happening at this very moment is really all that exists and all you can be sure of, so the wisest thing to do is stay here and experience life.

Do not pursue the past.
Do not lose yourself in the future.
The past no longer is.
The future has not yet come.
Looking deeply at life as it is
in the very here and now,
the practitioner dwells
in stability and freedom.

This doesn't mean we should throw away our calendars, that we shouldn't expect it to be warm in summer and cold in winter, or that we shouldn't prepare for an important meeting. But it does mean that every time we jot down an event or imagine a future scenario, a footnote should accompany that thought: life is full of surprises and anything can change at any moment. While it's smart to prepare ourselves for the probable, it's just as wise to stay open to the improbable. By getting into the habit of not having rigid expectations, of not grasping onto our hopes so tightly that we become dependent on them for our happiness, we can escape a lot of the pain of disappointment.

It's also wise to frequently remind ourselves that we never know what will make us happiest down the line. A friend can drag you to a party you're positive will be lame, and you can end up having the time of your life. You can spend a hundred dollars on a concert ticket to see your favorite band and they can put on a boring, uninspired show. You never know. So stay open. Nip your assumptions in the bud. And practice taking life as it comes, moment by moment.

Yes, No, and I Don't Care

Buddha recognized that there are three ways that we typically react to an experience. We either like it, dislike it, or don't care about it. When we like something, we want to possess it, get more of it, make it last. When we dislike something, we want to get rid of it, avoid it, get it over with. When we don't care, we want to ignore it. He felt that these three reactions cause an enormous amount of suffering. If we can't get what we want, we're unhappy. If we're stuck with something we don't want, we're unhappy. If we're forced to deal with something we don't care about, we're unhappy. He thought it would be much wiser to accept what we experience without wanting it to be any different and without wanting more or less of it. To not want anything is the definition of bliss. Unfortunately, we usually have to be floating in a turquoise ocean off the shores of a Caribbean island or cuddling with the man of our dreams after a wild night of sex to have that completely content, I-wouldn't-want-to-be-anywhere-else feeling—and even those periods of bliss come to an end. The only way to achieve constant contentment is to find a way to sustain a feeling of satisfaction no matter where you are or who you're with. This is extremely difficult and only the most devout and hard-working Buddhists are able to pull it off all of the time. But anyone can benefit from taking a crack at the Buddhist technique for accomplishing it. Of course, as always, the main way to get there is to meditate. When you meditate with the specific purpose of continually bringing yourself back to the present and focusing on the here and now—not daydreaming, not remembering, not planning, not analyzing, not complaining, just *being*—you're training yourself to be content with the present moment. Aside from meditating, you can also work on breaking the habit any time you feel a desire or dissatisfaction during your daily life. Instead of altering the situation right away, wait a while. Hang out and just deal. Be bored. Be hungry. Be hot. Tolerate a yucky smell, or an annoying sound. Continue talking to someone you find completely uninteresting. Force yourself to face something you'd usually just run away from. After several minutes go ahead and make whatever change you want. By riding out an unpleasant situation, you learn that you don't always need to chase or avoid things. You already have the ability to be OK no matter what's going on around you; you just need to wake up and realize it.

~ All Roads Lead to Nirvana ~

Every school of Buddhism is based on *the four noble truths* and *the eightfold path*, but as Buddha's philosophy became established as a belief system, many cultures chose to adorn it with religious trappings—symbols, rituals, prayers, temples, myths, etc. Some combined Buddha's philosophy with ideas from already existing religions. Others colored Buddha's words to match the politics of the time. The result is that there now exist dozens of different Buddhist traditions. Some fans of Buddha find that structure and ceremony help them to better grasp and live by his philosophies. Others, especially in the West, find complicated rituals and symbols distracting and unnecessary. Rather than criticize each other for being "right" or "wrong," the great majority of Buddhists accept that different methods work for different people and they have a great deal of respect for one another. Never once in the course of human history have two schools of Buddhism gone to war over conflicting beliefs.

The following are a few of the main schools of Buddhism. They range from the completely logical to the totally mystical.

INSIGHT MEDITATION

Defining characteristic: Practicality

Insight meditation is also becoming known as "Buddhism Without Beliefs," which is the title of a book by Stephen Batchelor, a highly respected British Buddhist teacher. It puts aside all Buddhist theories that can't be proven through personal experience and focuses only on the logical aspects of suffering and the process of alleviating suffering.

ZEN

Defining characteristic: Austerity

Zen Buddhists use the practice of sitting meditation to grasp the reality that "now" is the only time, "here" is the only place, and "form is emptiness, emptiness is form." The atmosphere in a *zendo* (a room devoted to group sitting meditation that is presided over by a Zen master) is serene, with no unnecessary objects present. Depending on the *zendo*, some teachers are kind and gentle, others are stern—whacking people who fall asleep with sticks.

THERAVADA

Defining characteristic: Formality

Theravadan Buddhists strive to adhere very strictly to the fundamental teachings of Buddha. Monks are revered highly, temples are sacred, and rules and rituals abound. Theravadan meditation focuses mainly on impermanence and on loving-kindness to all living things.

TIBETAN

Defining characteristic: Karma

Tibetan Buddhists believe that beings achieve enlighten-ment over the course of many lifetimes by working to improve their karma (their moral scoreboard, so to speak). Being wise, compassionate, and generous creates good karma. Being igno-rant, cruel, and selfish creates bad karma. Each time a person is reincarnated, the body and conditions into which they are born reflect the present state of their karma. A person reaches nirvana when she has perfected her karma and therefore breaks the cycle of needing to be reborn.

PURE LAND

Defining characteristic: Faith

The Pure Land concept of Buddha is that he is more of a god than a man. Practitioners of Pure Land Buddhism rely on their faith in the power and will of Buddha to achieve enlight-enment. The focus is on chanting as a way to bring out the Buddha within them, as well as on practicing compassion.

NICHIREN

Defining characteristic: Chanting

Nichiren was a rebellious Japanese teacher who thought that a highly mystical Buddhist text known as the *Lotus Sutra* was superior to all others. Like Pure Land Buddhists, Nichiren Buddhists rely more on faith and prayer than logic or experience. Nichiren Buddhists use a chant that translates to "Homage to the *Lotus Sutra*" as the primary means of improving their karma.

3

Space to Chill

Don't you love lounging in a Zen-inspired spa? As you walk through the door, it's as if you just downed a cocktail and took a quick dip in a pool. The tension in your neck and shoulders begins to melt, your breathing gets slower and deeper, your mind instantly stops racing. When you look around the room, you notice that it's spacious, uncluttered, and full of soft light. The atmosphere is grounded with rocks and natural tones like soothing blues and healing greens, and energized by fresh-smelling plants and moving water. Overall, it feels balanced in some indescribable way, which makes *you* feel balanced just by being there.

This is what our homes should feel like. Life is crazy enough everywhere else, so our apartments or houses should be nurturing, calm, rejuvenating places. Unfortunately, our busy, hectic lifestyles easily lead to an incredible mess. We run in and out, and barely have time to notice where we're putting anything, much less ponder whether it's in the right place. And without money to burn, redecorating isn't exactly high on our list of priorities. But transforming our pads into Zen havens, as difficult as it may seem, takes a lot less effort than we might think—and next to no cash, thanks to the Buddhist sensibility that less is more. The emphasis of a Zen environment is on simplicity and openness, which means there should be only a handful of meaningful objects in each room beyond the things that you actually need (plus the useless stuff that you'd rather die than part with). It's the opposite of the "cozy" Western aesthetic, by which we surround ourselves with lots of things as a way to feel comforted and secure. From a Buddhist perspective, material things provide only a superficial, and not very satisfying, sense of security. And the more stuff we have, the harder it is to keep it in order. As our surroundings get out of control, we start to *feel* out of control.

Nonattachment to material things—go ahead and buy them and enjoy them, but don't depend on them for happiness—is a central aspect of Buddhism, and applying it to our homes can reveal some interesting truths. We often keep things not because we need them but because we're attached to them for some other reason—whether it's nostalgia, the desire to project a certain image to others, or to feed our own egos. Nostalgia isn't all that bad but image-building is a habit worth breaking. My own decorating crutch is books. I'm constantly bringing them home and piling them up on every shelf and flat surface in my apartment. Though I tell myself that this is because they contain information that I might need or want to refer to at any moment, much of my attachment to books reflects my attachment to the idea of myself as a well-read person. The reality is that only a small fraction of my library is really useful. The rest is just propping up my self-confidence. That realization alone is enough to help loosen my ties to it. Clearly, I don't need more books—I need more self-confidence. With that understanding, the idea of donating them to a library makes me feel better than keeping them, and that's exactly what I'm going to do. I swear!

Create Cloud Nine

If you're interested in trying meditation, the best way to start is to clear out a corner of a room and designate it as a place where you can always get a break from your thoughts and emotions, no matter how intense they may seem. Keep two cushions (one small and thick for under your rear end, one large and thin for under your knees or ankles) in this corner at all times. If you'd like, you can also create a tiny shrine for inspiration. Place a candle and a tiny statue of Buddha on the floor next to the cushion or on a table or shelf nearby. Write this quote on a piece of paper and place it next to the statue. Read it whenever you need to rejuvenate:

> "Are you quiet?
> Quiet your body.
> Quiet your mind.
> By your own efforts
> Waken yourself,
> Watch yourself,
> And live joyfully."

Yes, it does take time and energy to rethink, simplify, and organize your surroundings, but consider it an investment in your own well-being that will have both instant and long-term benefits. It's counterintuitive, but a week spent nurturing your home can give you as much of a sense of satisfaction and happiness as a week spent lying on the beach. If you don't have a week, set aside a few weekends over the next couple of months to transform your pad. (P.S. A great perk of Zen redecorating is that you'll end up *making* money from all the things you sell, and feeling warm and fuzzy about all the things you give away.)

OWN LESS TO STRESS LESS

Chances are that most of us don't even have a decent idea of what we own. Can you name everything that is in the bottom drawer of your desk? What about the top shelf of your bedroom closet? If you don't even know something is there, do you really need it?

Probably not. It's taking up space and contributing to an overall feeling of clutter. Reducing what we own to just those things that we use and/or enjoy on a regular, ongoing basis is the first step to giving a house or apartment a Zen overhaul. For instant catharsis, start with the places to which you give very little thought, such as those storage nooks and crannies that you throw things into precisely because you don't need them. Get in there and purge! Either sell or give away any of the following:

- clothes and shoes that you haven't worn for more than a year
- sports equipment that never sees the light of day
- things you bought on trips or vacations that turned out to be tacky and/or useless
- broken stuff that you thought you'd fix but never did and never will
- gifts that you don't like but are keeping out of a sense of obligation
- seasonal decorations that you never bother to put up
- stuff you keep around because, hey, it could be used to make a Halloween costume
- leftover arts and crafts supplies from age-old projects
- chairs that are never sat on
- cushions, curtains, sheets, and decorations that don't match anything in your house
- out-of-date magazines
- dishes, glasses, pots, and kitchen appliances that you never use
- empty picture frames
- out of fashion jewelry and hair accessories
- canned food or booze that you don't even like
- books and movies that you hated
- pet supplies for pets that are no longer with us
- greeting cards that don't contain personal sentiments of any importance
- information in paper form that you could easily get online (recycle all those phone books!)

If the thought of sorting through all of this stuff is too daunting, just throw it all into double-ply garbage bags and drive it to the nearest Salvation Army. Beware of thoughts like "This could be worth something someday," "That might come back in fashion," or "Maybe I'll wish I had an ice-cream maker next summer." What you gain from having clean, open space in your home is worth losing things that have a 2 percent chance of being valuable somewhere down the line. Have faith that if you need something in the future, you will have the means to get it. The fact that we live in a society in which we can buy anything anytime is a very good reason *not* to horde. Let other people who will use, enjoy, or really need these things at this moment have them.

Once you've started this process, you won't want to stop. You can almost feel the weight of ownership leaving your shoulders. The sight of an only half-full drawer or closet is surprisingly liberating. You can actually see what's in there and get to it easily. You become aware of what you have, and that awareness gives an incredible sense of control. There's no more clutter, no more confusion, no more stuff clogging up your space, preventing air and energy from circulating. You can breathe!

Just be careful that all that extra space doesn't compel you to go out and buy new and different things that you don't need. Strive to become discriminate about what you bring into your home. Acknowledge that each object, item of clothing, handbag, knick-knack, electronic gadget, movie, or whatever you buy or otherwise acquire is yet another attachment that you're creating. When I have an impulse to buy something I try to wait a minimum of twenty-four hours before putting down my money—which I succeed in doing only about half the time. This way I'm sure that it's something I really will use and enjoy in a significant way. Most of the time, the next day rolls around and I realize that I could care less about having it. That impulse to buy, to possess, is very strong. As a woman, I think it's in my bones to hunt and gather. But, like any other urge, it can be overcome with awareness and a little honesty.

· · · · · · ·

Mini-Meditation: Mind Like Fire

Place a candle on the ground four feet in front of you and watch the flame as it flickers around the wick. Notice that the flame has no real, permanent shape. It changes countless times per second. Consider that the flame didn't exist until you created a spark with a match and then provided it with the fuel and oxygen necessary to sustain it. But though the flame's existence is dependent on those elements, it is also something very separate from them. This one flame has the power to grow larger and burn down entire cities, but it might also go out at any moment. Meditate on the ways that your own consciousness has the same characteristics of a flame.

FIX THE F-ING THING!

Little problems in your home can drain your happiness like a tiny leak, one drop at a time. I'm talking about pesky, frustrating things that, because they're so small, you're barely even aware of. For example, the piece of carpet under my computer chair. The carpet was there because it was the only thing stopping my chair from rolling across the slanted wooden floor into the kitchen. It was supposed to prevent aggravation, not cause it. But every time the wheels of my chair ventured beyond the edges of the carpet, they got stuck, and I'd have to get up, lift the chair (which is heavy and has all these moving parts), and put it back onto the rug. It stressed me out every time. For months I was aggravated by this problem, but never once did I devote any time to trying to correct it. It felt too insignificant to warrant the effort. Finally, after lifting up the awkward chair for what must have been the hundredth time, I started screaming obscenities at no one and decided to do something about it. I stepped back for a look, and realized that because I usually roll back and forth, and not side-to-side, if I just turned the rectangular carpet ninety degrees, the problem would be solved. It was that easy. And by making the change, I saved myself what must have added up to at least three annoying minutes a day.

I'll bet there are dozens of little annoyances in your living space right this second, from a hook that a towel or coat is always falling off of, to an extension cord that's constantly tripping you up, to a drawer that doesn't close properly. These little nuisances can mean the difference between a good mood and a bad mood—a happy, generous you and a cranky, selfish you—on any given day. So get out a piece of paper and when you notice a pinprick of frustration, write down what caused it and take a second to cook up a simple solution.

You might also want to investigate some books about feng shui, an Asian art that focuses on how objects should be placed for the most ease of use. Some feng shui tips are a little nutty, like using mirrors to deflect bad energy from nearby traffic, but others just make good sense. A few that I always incorporate into my home are placing furniture and beds so that a person using them can easily see the doorway, not placing a mirror directly across from the bed so you don't scare the crap out of yourself when you sit up in the middle of the night, and placing frequently used appliances (lamps, the telephone, the coffeemaker) on the right side of a table, desk, or countertop (or the left if you're left-handed) so that they're more easily reached. And this is a random thing that has nothing to do with feng shui, but throw out socks and underwear that are so threadbare you'd be embarrassed if anyone ever saw them. True luxury is having exclusively A-list sock and lingerie drawers.

We all also have subtle habits that contribute to that feeling of being overwhelmed with stress. Not refilling the Brita pitcher even though we know there's only a quarter inch of water left after pouring the last glass, forgetting to charge our cell phones, letting paperwork pile up to the point where filing it becomes a monstrous task. We won't kick any of these habits overnight, but just becoming aware of them (and writing them down) helps us to do them less often, until eventually, filling up the Brita every time, always plugging in our phones when we're at home, and filing bills as soon as we pay them actually become habits. This is not sexy life-improvement, just realistic life-improvement.

Monks Gone Wild: Leaping Kitties

An isolated Buddhist monastery located in the politically volatile country Myanmar has become an unlikely hot spot for tourists. Unfortunately, people don't flock there to seek spiritual guidance. They go to see cats jump through hoops. The abbot of the monastery started caring for a few stray cats about ten years ago and eventually began training them as a way to pass the time. Since he first coaxed one to jump through a plastic hoop, other felines have followed suit, and the act has become a surprising form of entertainment for travelers and locals alike. In a 1999 article by the Associated Press, the then sixty-four-year-old abbot grumbled that "Nobody ever asks about Buddhism. They just come to see the cats."

AUTHENTIC ZEN LIVIN'

Just because a place has a few bamboo stalks, a pile of river stones, and a waterfall doesn't mean it is Zen. True Zen style is about simplicity and practicality. Meditation rooms are open, airy spaces with a single focal point, cushions to sit on, and not much else. Because of their simplicity, not in spite of it, they are some of the calmest, most relaxing places you could ever spend time in. The most beautiful meditation rooms also use natural elements such as rocks, water, and plants to add texture and color. They're luxurious and relaxing without any excess at all.

The first step to creating that kind of serenity in your space is to clarify the main purpose of each area in your house or apartment. The kitchen table, for example, is used for the preparation and eating of food, so there should only be things suited to that purpose on top of it. Anything else on the table—a purse, a stack of magazines, or whatever—will be distracting. You'll look at the table and feel a pang of disharmony. For the same reason, there shouldn't be anything having to do with food in your living room, work in your bedroom, or bathing in your kitchen. Even if you live in a studio apartment, there should be designated areas for eating, sleeping, working, and playing.

Sacred Symbols

The only time most people investigate the meaning of Buddhist symbols is when they're shopping for a cool tattoo. Here's what the following three ubiquitous images actually mean:

Yin and yang represent the natural duality of all things. Yin is the feminine element that represents darkness, receptivity, and softness. Yang is the male element that represents activity, light, and harshness. The small amount of the other contained in each is symbolic of the idea that each element carries the seed of its opposite and can therefore change into that opposite.

The Eyes of the Buddha see suffering in all directions and face it with compassion.

The lotus flower symbolizes the transformation of a selfish human being into an enlightened Buddha because of the way that it grows. The lotus takes root in the muck at the bottom of a pond but its stem rises up through the muddy water toward the sun, until its leaves and flowers blossom on the surface of the pond, pure and unaffected by the dirt below.

Once everything is in the area where it belongs, items should be arranged so that what you use every day is within the easiest reach. The things you use once a week should be on the next level of storage both up and down. Items you pull out once a month can go still higher and lower, and things that you use only once in a great while should be on the very top and bottom levels of storage. Stuff that you use several times a day, such as a bottle-opener or a hairbrush, should not be in a cabinet or drawer that you have to open and close, but instead should rest or hang alone in a convenient spot. By making these changes you reduce the amount of stress you encounter in having to search for things during your everyday routine.

Maybe your pad is already well organized, but just isn't easy on the eyes. Try taking a look at each room and mentally associating everything in it with one of the five basic elements: earth, water, air, metal, or fire. In feng shui and many other Asian traditions, human beings are thought to be a perfect balance of these five elements; environments that reflect this same balance make us happiest and most at ease. Use your instincts to figure out which element the things in your home most likely represent. Most couches, for example, are big, soft cushy things, which naturally make you think of earth. Plants, obviously, are earth, as are stones and wood and colors like green and brown. Hard, cold things like glass or electronics are metal, as are metallic colors. In addition to space, air can also be represented by very light, delicate objects, or things that move, like curtains that flow in the breeze. Water can be something obvious, like a fishbowl or a fountain; but it can also be anything that makes you think of rain or the ocean, as well as blue-green hues. Fire is light in the form of lamps, candles, and sunlight, and also red and orange shades. Trust your gut. Once you've assigned everything an element, take note as to whether there's an abundance of any one element in a particular room, or if any aren't represented at all. Then, using only things you already own, make an attempt to balance out the elements in the room, or come as close to a balance as you can. Here are some tips that might be helpful:

- Balance out areas with a lot of electronics or metal by placing green, leafy plants nearby.
- Hang colorful paintings on white walls and black-and-white photographs on colored walls.
- Create a single area in every room that your eyes will be naturally drawn to first.
- Store small, easily scattered things like coins or jewelry in solid, heavy containers.
- Place bright, colorful objects in dark corners.
- Don't pack bookshelves tightly. Leave open spaces.
- Use cool colors (whites, light blues, and greens) in rooms that get an excess of sunlight; use warm colors (reds, oranges, yellows) in rooms that are often cold.
- Your bedroom should be the simplest, sparest room in your house. There should be nothing in it that makes you think of work or stress.
- Mirrors are a good way to add metal to a room that has too much earth.
- A layer of stones in a small bowl makes a perfect soap dish and helps balance the element of water in the bathroom.
- A single flower or branch can be far more soothing to look at than a giant bouquet.

Remember that there should also be a balance between objects and the space around them. Overall, the room should feel spacious and air should seem to flow through it easily.

For more ideas and inspiration pay a visit to a real *zendo* to see how they use color, texture, and most of all, empty space to create an atmosphere of calm contemplation.

Sounds Good

One of the simplest changes you can make to add more *"om"* to your home is to stop using a blaring, beeping, buzzing alarm clock to wake up every morning. I use the alarm on my cell phone instead because it offers a wide range of far more soothing sounds to start the day with. No pleasant alarm option on your cell? Check to see if a watch that you already own might have one. If not, here's where I tell you to actually go out and buy something. If there's a single item that you shell out cash for in an attempt to live a calmer life, let it be an alarm clock that wakes you with a gentle, tinkling bell.

~ Find Bliss Online By . . . ~

. . . RAIDING A BUDDHIST LIBRARY

www.buddhanet.net
Buddha Net is a completely free and extensive online source for books on major Buddhist topics by famous teachers. It also offers audio tracks, movies, and more. If you download one thing from this site, make it *The Eightfold Path for the Householder* by Jack Kornfield. It's a wise, funny guide to the Buddhist way of life.

. . . BROWSING GORGEOUS IMAGES FROM TIBET

www.spirit-of-tibet.co.uk
British photographer Diane Barker gives us an intimate glimpse of Tibetan life with her portraits of Tibetan nomads, scenes from inside Buddhist temples, and images of Buddhists in exile in India and Nepal. The scenery is breathtaking, and the faces even more beautiful.

. . . TAKING A MEDITATION COURSE

www.wildmind.org
Bodhipaksa, a Buddhist teacher and author who lives in Portsmouth, New Hampshire, offers online meditation courses that are simple, laid-back, and inspiring.

. . . GETTING TIPS ON BEING GREEN

www.ecopractice.fwbo.org
This small, grassroots site is maintained by a handful of members of the Friends of Western Buddhism Order (www.fwbo.org), and presents a straightforward, five point agenda for living a more environmentally friendly life. The plan includes consuming less and conserving wildlife. The FWBO is also worth checking

out because it approaches Buddhist philosophy and practice from a very common-sense, practical perspective.

. . . Subscribing to an Ultramodern Buddhist Magazine

www.shambhalasun.com

The magazine of choice for urban Buddhists, the *Shambhala Sun* is a monthly publication that explores Buddhism as it applies to pop culture and everyday life. (Shambhala is a Western school of Buddhism that focuses mainly on awareness meditation and the core teachings of Buddha.) Past covers have featured Richard Gere and Jet Li.

. . . Starting a Buddhist Romance

www.dharmadate.com

If you're tired of all those materialistic, spiritually barren guys you're meeting at bars, check out this Buddhist dating site. Most of the singles here are Westerners into Zen meditation. I did a test search and found a very cute twenty-six-year-old artist from New York.

. . . Reading Essays by Current Teachers on Everyday Issues

www.urbandharma.org

Dedicated to Buddhism in America, Urban Dharma is a good resource for essays and articles about modern practice. Click on "Sutra" in the main menu to find some excellent basic texts and information about Buddhist history, including a clear, concise timeline.

———————————————

4

Bring Buddha to Work

As you've no doubt already figured out, most of what we were taught as kids about work and career was way off the mark. There is no such thing as the perfect job, a higher salary doesn't increase our self-esteem, and there isn't any profound happiness available at the top of the ladder that we can't achieve while standing on the first rung. As a journalist living in New York City, I've met actors, surgeons, professional athletes, organic farmers, yoga teachers, photographers, investment bankers, artists, news anchors, and fashion designers, and *everybody* always has a list of complaints about their careers that they can't wait to go on about. If it's not the hours that are the problem, it's the traveling; if it's not the traveling, it's the competition; if it's not the competition, it's the ass-kissing. And no matter how much money anyone makes, they *still* stress about cash. I once heard a male model—a single guy who didn't have a financial responsibility in the world—say that if his earnings didn't improve from a measly $160,000 a year, that was it, he was quitting. Clearly, having a "dream job" doesn't feel like a dream, and a ton of money doesn't make money issues disappear. Just reminding ourselves of that can in itself help us be happier with the job we already have. Another job would certainly be different, but that doesn't mean the positive-to-negative ratio would change much.

The reality that every job has negative aspects is not something we can change or fix, because *everything* and *everyone* has both positive and negative characteristics. This is not a pessimistic view; this is a basic law of the universe. As yin and yang symbolize, when any one condition exists, its opposite condition is nascent within it, poised to take over at any moment. Because of the reality of constant change, no one condition can last forever. So, inevitably, where there is interest or excitement, there will be boredom; where there is order, there will be confusion; where there is satisfaction, there will be discontent. If opposite conditions didn't exist, the world as we know it wouldn't work. A telephone is only functional because it rings at some times and doesn't at others. If it always rang or never rang, it would be useless. If you didn't have many moments of boredom during your day, you would never feel the sensation of becoming interested. Once we accept the principle of opposites, it doesn't have to drive us crazy. As we begin to expect negatives, they stop being so . . . well, negative. What I'm trying to say is that there's no avoiding the fact that your job will suck sometimes. It's guaranteed to, so there's nothing to fight against. If you try, you'll be fighting the nature of the universe, not your boss.

· · · · · · ·

Mini-Meditation: Love the Ones You're With

Jack Kornfield, a very talented Buddhist teacher and author of the book A Path with Heart, *once described a kind of loving-kindness meditation that he does when he finds himself on a bus full of people trying to ignore each other. Instead of giving in to the urge to isolate himself by reading or listening to music, he looks up and, without staring, glances at each person around him and sends them a quick mental message along the lines of "May you be well and happy." When I first read about this meditation idea, I thought it was unbearably corny. But then I tried it. And it's incredible how content and connected it made me feel. Now whenever I'm commuting and feeling particularly ornery, I do this meditation and without fail, it puts me in a better mood. And who knows, maybe it actually improves other people's lives as well. Try it the next time you're on a bus, the subway, a plane, or standing in line somewhere, and see if it has the same effect on you.*

Beyond the laws of constant change and yin and yang, Buddha had some very specific thoughts about how we can be happy with our jobs. It may be twenty-five-hundred-year-old advice, but it has enabled me to feel more passionate and positive about working than anything a career counselor or self-help book about colors and parachutes ever has.

YOU PROBABLY ALREADY HAVE THE "RIGHT" JOB

In his teachings on *right livelihood*, Buddha emphasizes that the only "wrong" job for any person is one that we know causes direct and serious harm to ourselves or other people. Alas, there's no escaping that most jobs cause harm to some living things, either directly or indirectly. In order to print books we have to kill trees and pollute the environment. To grow corn we have to kill bugs, rodents, and weeds. To design Web sites we have to use electricity that depletes natural resources. Depressing, isn't it? But at least there are degrees of harm. Obviously someone who works for a weapons factory is directly involved in killing people. A person who deals heroine is also causing direct harm. Someone who works for a liquor distributor, on the other hand, might be a little more confused about whether they're causing direct harm. And what about those who make matches or knives or other things that people sometimes use to harm themselves or others? In these dark-to-light-gray areas, what matters is only how we feel about our jobs deep down in our guts. Most of us could make a list of ways in which our jobs help people and bring them happiness, as well as some ways that they might cause stress or unhappiness. If your second list is considerably longer than your first, you will go to bed at night feeling uneasy about your life and yourself, no matter how much money you make or how desperately you think you need the job. To achieve greater happiness in your life, you should get out of that job, even if it means going on unemployment.

Those of us who can name a few harmful side effects of the industry we work in, but feel that the positive attributes of our jobs far outnumber them, need to allow ourselves to feel more satisfaction from that fact alone. Here we are, contributing something positive to society, but while we know it on some level, we seldom remind ourselves of it, or get any happiness from it. Why? Adding to the overall well-being of a society can and should be a huge source of contentment. But recognizing that to be true and allowing ourselves to benefit from that recognition would require the very brave act of defying the messages that television, movies, magazines, and advertisements send about what makes a person's job worthwhile. There's endless talk in our culture about "moving up," "status," and "making it." People with VIP titles get respect and people who make minimum wage get pitied. And in spite of the fact that we see people "at the top" such as Michael Jackson and Martha Stewart encountering intense misery, we still retain the illusion that a better, more important, more exciting, more profitable job would bring us a greater sense of satisfaction. If we can see past that illusion, pop that bubble of complete BS, forget everything our college career counselors ever told us, we can start looking at our current jobs as having an enormous amount of potential for creating satisfaction. Even if everyone around us is convinced that rock star is a better job than baker, that doesn't mean we have to hold the same conviction. Buddha encouraged his followers to be intellectual rebels, to be the few who grasp the truth of reality, and are happier as a result.

Meditate. Live purely. Be quiet. Do your work with mastery. Like the moon, come out from behind the clouds! Shine.

This doesn't mean you shouldn't take a better paying job or a more interesting or more glamorous one if it is offered to you. By all means, climb that ladder. But keep reading to find out why you don't necessarily need to move up or make bank in order to have a job that gives you joy.

BUDDHIST SECRETS TO OCCUPATIONAL BLISS

Here is something that we often fail to notice: it's not the nature of our job that makes us happiest, it's working hard that give us pleasure. The moments when we're dissatisfied with our jobs are usually when we're doing our work in a half-assed way, or not at all—we're procrastinating, unfocused, worrying about getting it done, confused about what we're even trying to do, or multitasking to the point of madness. But when we're actually fully engaged in a single aspect of our work, no matter what the work is, we develop this sort of happy buzz. A psychologist named Mihaly Csikszentmihalyi (yup, that's how to spell it) wrote a book about that buzz called *Flow: The Psychology of Optimal Experience*, which is pretty much a scientific take on the Buddhist practice of mindfulness. Said simply, the best way to be happier with your job is to *get into it*. Don't just sit there at your desk, or allow yourself to go on automatic pilot. Really be there and put true effort into completing the task at hand to the best of your ability. Alas, getting into that optimal zone can be tricky. In spite of the fact that mindful, high-energy work feels amazing, we seem to have a weird instinct to avoid it like the plague, hence all the daydreaming and procrastinating. In our work as in all sectors of our lives, it's as if our minds are wacky monkeys who are most content sitting quietly on branches, carefully contemplating the leaves and sky, yet they continue to want to swing around the jungle at random, even though it makes them dizzy, exhausted, and grumpy. Taming those monkeys—our minds—is the secret to achieving the deepest kind of satisfaction.

You'll Get There Eventually

It's amazing how your commute can suck the life out of you. You leave the house freshly showered, unwrinkled, optimistic, and by the time you get to work you're pissy, exhausted, and have given at least one stranger the finger. Use these ideas to make getting there a little more relaxing and a little less infuriating:

- Cover the clock on your dashboard with a sticker or piece of electrical tape. The fact that you're on your way is all that matters.
- Listen to dharma talks on CD that will soothe your soul (my favorite is *From Fear to Fearlessness*, by Pema Chödrön); borrow cheesy action or romance audiobooks from the library or listen to some of your favorite books from childhood being read out loud.
- If traffic isn't moving and you can spare a few minutes, take an exit off the highway or turn off the main road

and cruise a few side streets to get a better idea of the neighborhoods you're passing every day and night.
- Bring a tape recorder and dictate cassette-letters to friends you've been meaning to call or write to. Your grandmother would love one.
- Practice thinking good thoughts about the people around you—especially the ones who are driving or acting like idiots—to help strengthen your compassion reflex.

THE JOY OF GETTING INTO IT

Getting ourselves into prime work mode is a lot like preparing for sitting meditation. It starts with positioning our bodies best for what it is we're trying to do. The lazier and sloppier your posture is, the lazier and sloppier your mind will feel. Don't slump or stand too rigidly. Have an energized body, but a calm one. Feel your feet rooted into the ground; if you're sitting, feel your backside solid on the chair. Imagine that a string is attached to the crown of your head and is pulling your whole body upward. When your body feels energized and focused, it will be easier for your mind to follow suit. Now take a few deep breaths to bring yourself into the moment. Feel the air pass in and out of your nose. Do this several times. When you feel present in your body, tell yourself exactly what it is you want to get done and take a moment to visualize the steps between beginning and completing that task. Now begin.

Every time you feel your mind wandering beyond the task you're trying to complete, readjust your posture, take a few more mindful breaths, and then refocus your mind on the project. Remember, you're taming a monkey, so expect him to be a little unruly. But no matter what he's up to, you can always bring him back where he belongs by checking your posture and breathing, and refocusing. You'll find that there will be stretches of time when the monkey behaves, you stay involved with what you're doing, and you start getting results. And you'll feel good during and after those moments. You'll get a little joy from your work. After one or two hours you might need to get up and take a walk or eat a snack to rejuvenate, but then you can get right back to it by applying the right posture, right breath, right mindfulness, and right effort. The more you do it, the better you'll get at it, and the more you'll enjoy your day.

SMALL ACCOMPLISHMENTS ARE WHAT IT'S ALL ABOUT

A friend of mine is a fact-checker at an academic journal that covers international politics. She's always telling me how boring her job is, how depressing it is to sit in a dusty corner office with no windows and look up foreign words all day long, as the rest of the world passes her by. But then there are times when her eyes light up, her voice is full of life, and she's clearly psyched about her work. It happens every time she tells a story about a random piece of information that she was able to track down by surfing the Internet for two days, calling half a dozen people, and finally getting the answer from some PhD in Moscow. By the way she talks about it, you'd think she was describing digging for treasure and striking gold. It doesn't matter that the nature of the information is often dull as dishwater; it's doing her job well that makes her feel fulfilled. It's funny how every single one of us has the inherent desire to do our best.

You've probably heard advice along the lines of breaking up your long-term goals into small steps a million times before, but here's a reason to do it that has nothing to do with achieving the big "money and status" prize at the end—which we can never be sure will materialize, anyway. We should follow this advice because every time we face a small task and complete it successfully, our reward centers get a happy jolt. And if we can have dozens of happy jolts all day long simply by doing our jobs, we'll end up enjoying life a hell of a lot more. All it takes is defining a task, facing it straight on (posture, breath, focus), getting into it, and finishing. And *ding, ding, ding!* We're a little more satisfied than we were before. I know it sounds small scale, but life, in reality, is both small scale and massive at the same time. If you want to achieve happiness on a massive, cosmic scale all at once, join a monastery. When you get there the Buddhist master will hand you a broom and tell you to go mindfully sweep the floor.

Monks Gone Political: The Ultimate Sacrifice

On June 11, 1963, seventy-three-year-old Buddhist monk Thich Quang Duc protested the Vietnam war by setting himself on fire in a busy intersection of Saigon. He sat motionless in meditation posture as the flames engulfed him. David Halberstam, a *New York Times* reporter, wrote: "As he burned he never moved a muscle, never uttered a sound, his outward composure in sharp contrast to the wailing people around him." In the following months, other monks would repeat his action in the hope of helping to publicize the suffering of the Vietnamese people. The photos had a powerful effect on the American public and helped add to the anti-war sentiment. There is now a monastery honoring Thich Quang Duc in Melbourne, Australia.

MAKE INNER GROWTH YOUR GOAL

If work were just a simple matter of working hard and getting things done, deriving pleasure from it wouldn't be so hard. Unfortunately, there are things like commuting, 8 a.m. meetings, power-tripping bosses, and annoying coworkers, not to mention fluorescent lights, bad coffee, stagnant air, and never enough pens to go around. You may be lucky enough to work in a place where everyone is cool and your offices are swank, but most of us have to deal with at least one person who gets under our skin, and a few frustrating factors when it comes to getting to, or being in, the office. In the book *Work as a Spiritual Practice*, author Lewis Richmond points out that these frustrations are what give us an opportunity to turn our jobs into something much more important than a way to make money or feel useful. Work is a like an obstacle course for your character, a place rigged with little hurdles and pitfalls that you can either soar over or slam into. So let's say that you walk into the office kitchen and there's the boss's secretary, Marge, and she's doing all the things that you can't stand. She left the milk out after making her coffee, she's singing show tunes at the top of her lungs despite the fact that people in nearby offices are trying to work, and when she sits down at the table to noisily slurp her split-pea soup, she simultaneously starts clipping her nails.

In his book, Lewis describes your mind like the gears of a car with first, second, third, fourth, (and maybe fifth), reverse, and neutral. At the mere sight of Marge, you may immediately shift into third gear—which, for you, is anger. Lewis suggests that when you encounter a Marge at work, you try to catch yourself shifting into a reflex gear such as anger, hostility, irritation, boredom, frustration, or whatever, and gently imagine shifting out of that gear and back into neutral. Idle there until those first powerful feelings begin to dissipate. Then try and shift into a lower gear that will actually improve the situation, such as smiling, putting the milk away, and deciding to eat lunch at your desk. Even if the annoyance is caused by an inanimate object—for instance, when your computer keeps freezing up or crashing—try the same method. Shift into neutral and just sit in idle, as emotionless as possible. When you've put some distance between you and the negative feeling, try to make a positive change—like calling in the IT guy and letting him deal with the problem while you pop out for a latté.

After all, it's your ability to remain calm and content in the face of stress and unpleasantness that leads to real and lasting bliss. It doesn't require changing your situation, but rather improving your ability to tolerate and handle your situation. Many Buddhist teachers would say that a pain-in-the-ass job is the *perfect* place to learn how to be happy. Meanwhile, of course, we'll continue to view our work as a source of money, friendships, and direction and purpose in our lives, and that's all helpful and good. We should just try to remember, as often as we can, that it's just another part of life in which we encounter challenges to happiness and serenity and have a chance to overcome them.

A Cerebral Way to Save

When you find yourself lusting after anything you can't afford, take a step back and imagine that the dress you're salivating over is already in your closet, that the pair of earrings in the glass case is actually sitting in your jewelry box, the ten-CD set is already gathering dust next to your stereo. There it is, in your life. Now, what's changed? What's better? What's different? If you can imagine it having a major impact on your permanent happiness, go ahead and buy it. But, otherwise, why not walk away with the pleasure of not having yet another thing you don't need.

THREE WAYS MONEY CAN MAKE YOU HAPPY

1. There's no doubt that possessing things that you like and that make your life easier and more comfortable is a real source of pleasure. A big, comfy couch, reliable car, soft bed, good coffeemaker—they won't make you feel a deep sense of love or compassion, but they will give you a nice place to sit, a method of transportation, a better night's sleep, and a tasty cup of java. Buddha never suggested that people shouldn't own things. (When he ditched all of his belongings and headed into the forest to meditate it was to ensure that he was free of attachment to material things. And, sure enough, he was.) His only suggestion was that we shouldn't become so attached to our possessions that the thought of losing them, or not being able to get more stuff in the future, causes us to suffer. And we should never be under the illusion that having a lot of stuff makes us a better, more attractive, more interesting, or more worthwhile person because, again, that will lead to all sorts of stress and worry about whether we'll ever have enough. But if we can possess things lightly, enjoying them but not holding on to them to dearly, then having money to buy material goods can be a wonderful thing.

2. An even better benefit of earning some green is to become completely free of debt. Freedom from debt is a much more profound source of pleasure than the sound of a new stereo or the feel of a new pair of shoes. The knowledge that you don't owe anyone anything, that you're not causing anyone else or yourself suffering by not paying your bills, is intensely liberating. In his lessons to non-monastic people, Buddha often stressed the joy of debtlessness and urged people with jobs to make it a priority so that they could be free from any blame or fault on account of money. In the past I've owed so much to Visa and Mastercard that I felt as if I were in a hole I couldn't get out of. Every time I reached for my wallet to pay for groceries or buy a pack of gum, I felt the pressure of that debt on my shoulders. That kind of pressure really sucks. If you've managed to come to a place in your life where you don't owe, then pat yourself on the back and take some serious joy in that accomplishment. Revel in your financial freedom. If you have balances on your cards and outstanding loans, let paying them off be your first financial priority so that you can treat yourself to the good life without any guilt.

3. Lastly, money gives you an opportunity to help other people. To give to charity, to support humanitarian political groups, to buy a struggling Visa-strangled friend a nice dinner. Money, when used wisely, can and does effect positive change. It can be especially satisfying if you donate cash to local causes and you get to see improvements being made. Whether you can witness your donations in action or not, always try to give with an open heart and no strings attached. Consider your ability to give a financial gain, not a loss. And, in case you didn't know, black-tie charity events are massive pickup scenes.

If you knew what I know about the power of giving, you would not let a single meal pass without sharing it in some way.

REMEMBER THAT A "CAREER" ISN'T ALL IT'S CRACKED UP TO BE

As a final word on work and happiness, I urge you to ask yourself who it is you're working for and why. Many of us cook up ambitious career plans and bust our butts trying to get one promotion after another, not because it's what would make us happiest, but because we want our parents to be proud, we want to be seen as a more attractive romantic partner, we're trying to impress our friends, or we're just competing for the sake of competition—to be the best, the richest, the most important. If your life is out of balance because you work too much, and the reason behind it is anything other than your own happiness and peace of mind, then you should find a way to slow down and give attention to other parts of your life that will bring you joy. When I give myself that advice, my brain immediately screams "But I can't! I need to put money in my IRA! I need to have enough in case I get sick! I need to put a down-payment on a condo!" But none of those needs are about this moment, right now, the only moment that truly matters. It's good to put aside some money for the future, but if you focus most of your time and energy on constantly preparing for the next phase of life, you're making a grave mistake.

In 2000, in order to go freelance and live a less structured, less conventional life, I quit a magazine job that provided me with health insurance, a good salary, respect from my peers, and an impressive title for my parents to brag about. As a result, five years later, I have no idea what I'll be doing next month, let alone next year, or five years from now. And instead of that being a source of stress, it's almost always a source of curiosity and excitement (I admit that once in a while I freak out, but I always come to my senses and realize that there's no such thing as job security no matter where you work). There's something about sitting back and letting life happen—while simultaneously trying to do your best at everything you take on—that feels like the most natural, easy way to be.

~ A Brief History of Tibet ~

Tibet, sometimes called "The Roof of the World," is located in a mountainous region between India and China that soars sixteen thousand feet above sea level. Throughout early history, Tibet was divided into many warring kingdoms and the main religion, called Bön, was rooted in animalism and shamanism. The country was unified in 641 AD by a powerful king who married a Buddhist princess from Nepal. To please his queen he built 108 Buddhist temples across the region. But Buddhism did not become the dominant religion of Tibet until 774, when King Trisong Detsen invited a Tantric Buddhist mystic named Padmasambhava (also known as Guru Rinpoch) to come to Tibet and become the country's religious leader. Padmasambhava combined aspects of Bön and Tantra to form what would become Tibetan Buddhism.

In the tenth century, Tibet was conquered by the armies of Genghis Khan, and it was decided that the government of Tibet would be run by a spiritual figure or *lama*. The third of these spiritual leaders was declared to be the Dalai Lama (which translates to "teacher of an ocean of wisdom"), a divine being who is continuously reincarnated. When a Dalai Lama dies, the search for the child who has inherited his spirit begins. Sometimes several prospective children are found and they are put through tests in which they are asked to identify possessions of the previous Dalai Lama. The child who successfully chooses the Dalai Lama's things is believed to be the bearer of his spirit.

Beginning in the eighteenth century, there were several attempts by communist China to infiltrate and take over Tibet, but the only successful invasion occurred in 1950 when the People's Liberation Army attacked the almost defenseless country. Over one million Tibetans were killed and all but a few of the country's six thousand monasteries were destroyed. Six years later, after a failed Tibetan revolution, the fourteenth and current Dalai Lama, His Holiness Tenzin Gyatso, was forced to flee to India where he now resides in exile in the town of Dharamsala. The political atmosphere in China-controlled Tibet remains oppressive. Buddhists who openly sympathize with the Dalai Lama are frequently imprisoned. Many have been tortured and killed.

The Dalai Lama travels all over the world in an attempt to spread the Buddhist principals of compassion and nonviolence, as well as to gain support for the liberation of Tibet. To find out more about his teachings and Tibet, go to www.tibet.com.

5
Dating Dharma

B uddha once said that to have fifty loves is to have fifty woes, because when you care about someone, you naturally fret over that person's well-being and become fearful of losing him or her. The flipside, of course, is that if you have fifty loves, you have fifty wonderful sources of happiness and comfort. But forget about the other forty-nine. It's that *one* romantic love at the center of our lives that gets most of our time and attention, and causes most of our bliss and misery. Even if we're lucky enough to meet a great match, the yin and yang nature of love guarantees that it won't always be a walk in the park. It's inevitable that anything that provides us with such incredible amounts of pleasure and satisfaction is bound to serve up an equal amount of stress. Sometimes in a relationship it seems as if tension builds for no reason at all, until it's eventually released in the form of ridiculous debates that escalate into full-blown brawls. Which happens to me all the time. Last time the fight was over *King Kong*—I thought it was a sexist movie, my boyfriend thought I was nuts. We ended up arguing in the middle of the street about the phallic symbolism of the Empire State Building. Welcome to the bizarre nature of relating to the opposite sex.

Since a certain amount of tension and conflict go with the territory, the most successful couples aren't those who are deliriously happy all of the time—they're the ones who have learned how to ride out the rough spots. Like people on a raft on a choppy ocean, they accept that every relationship will experience dips and swells, so they don't get an urge to jump overboard every time the going gets bad. Similarly, the most successful daters manage to maintain perspective when a guy doesn't call, commit, or come through in any other way—they just consider him another Mr. Wrong along the road to finding Mr. Right (because, obviously, Mr. Right *will* call again and again). The big challenge is to establish a Buddhist state of level-headedness and compassion in the midst of so much powerful emotion.

This is a major challenge to pull off most of the time, and downright impossible to do *all* of the time. But if we can maintain a little more awareness, compassion, and perspective when our hearts are thumping wildly in our chests, we can smooth out some pretty big bumps in what will hopefully be a long and happy love life.

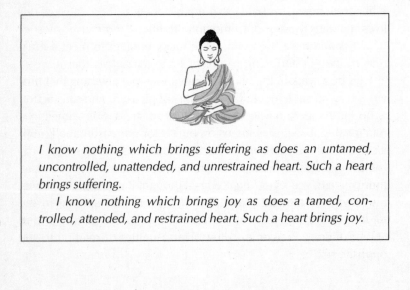

I know nothing which brings suffering as does an untamed, uncontrolled, unattended, and unrestrained heart. Such a heart brings suffering.

I know nothing which brings joy as does a tamed, controlled, attended, and restrained heart. Such a heart brings joy.

FIRST, HEAL YOUR HEART

In the preceding quote, Buddha warned of the painful risks of having an "untamed, uncontrolled, unattended, and unrestrained heart." In the twenty-first century, we call that having relationship issues. Almost everyone has a few—there's fear of commitment, lack of confidence, trouble communicating, overdependence, obsessive crushing, always dating men who treat you poorly, and that's just for starters. In order to tame our hearts, we need to know what our particular issues are, explore what's lurking behind them, and learn to control our often unwise responses to them. Very tall order. But I'm living proof that meditation can help make it happen. I hope that airing my dirty laundry will shed some light on exactly how.

As you may have guessed from the snake-girl fiasco in Chapter Two, my big relationship issue has always been jealousy—nagging, awful, embarrassing jealousy. If it's never been a problem for you, you're one lucky woman. In the past, the green-eyed monster has not only made me miserable, it's also caused me to be unfair to my boyfriends (by accusing them of being untrustworthy), nasty to other women (because I saw them as competition instead of people), and emotionally needy (I needed constant reassurance). Yuck.

At the root of this jealousy was the usual suspect: a philandering high school boyfriend who left me unable to trust guys further than I could throw them. Your basic slimeball, every time I looked the other way, he'd be chatting up another girl in that oh-so-familiar pose: his hand resting on the wall behind her head. We fought about his incessant flirting and, finally, after finding him in a bedroom with his paws up a girl's shirt for the *third time*, I dumped him. Friends insisted that he was just one lying jerk, and that there were countless nice guys out there whom I actually could trust. But by then I had already trained my brain to be hypersensitive to any signs of potential infidelity. I imposed that sensitivity onto my next two boyfriends, in spite of the fact that they were loving, honest, and nothing at all like the slimeball. Each of them struggled in vain to convince me that I had nothing to worry about, but I wouldn't allow myself to trust them for fear that I'd be deceived again. I was so worried, I never opened up to them, and things eventually fell apart.

It took a full year of on-and-off honest meditation on my beliefs and fears about love to realize that my perceptions had become skewed, and that most of what I had seen as threatening behavior was just friendliness or, at the worst, harmless flirtation. The truth was that I could no longer trust my gut on this issue, because it was heavily biased. This was a hard thing to accept because we all naturally feel attached to our own judgments—we interpret something a certain way and think it's the truth, end of story. But questioning the validity of my overly-negative reactions was necessary before I could begin to battle my inner demon. When I carefully thought over what had happened in the past, there was no evidence that either of those innocent ex's had any intention to stray, and all the evidence in the world that I had overreacted on dozens of occasions.

When we reach the point at which our emotions begin to have unnecessary negative effects on our lives, it's time to take Buddha's advice and straighten out our hearts and heads. You can probably quickly pinpoint the hurtful events in your past that are the source of some false or overly pessimistic beliefs about men, love, or yourself that get in the way of a happy relationship. If you can't, it might be time to sit down and figure out who or what is at the root of your untamed heart. This type of meditation is about honing in on an aspect of your life—in this case boyfriends, dating, hooking up—and then surrendering to the thoughts and feelings that arise. You should control your mind slightly, bringing it back to the topic of your romantic past when it strays to something else, but otherwise let it roam freely. You may avoid painful memories the first few times you meditate in this way, but avoidance will probably give way to some interesting discoveries sooner than you think.

A quick but inspiring example of meditation success: A friend of mine who's never had confidence around guys began to spend some time in sitting meditation with the goal of confronting her insecurities. She had more than a hunch as to where they began. At the age of thirteen, awkward and with braces, her aunt told her that she "wasn't the kind of girl guys go for." That comment had been etched in her mind for fourteen years. The Buddha's teachings about impermanence helped her to rethink the nature of that insensitive, off-the-cuff comment, and she began to let go of it, as well as other perceptions about herself that she realized were damaging to her happiness and love life. As a result of her new understanding, she ended up developing a kind of alarm system. Now, when she starts feeling down about her supposed lack of sex appeal, she pictures her aunt and mentally gives her the finger. Not exactly a Zen technique, but it works for her.

Even if you can't put a face, date, or location on the source of your negative hang-ups about guys and dating, you can still overcome them. Thoughts like "I'm not sexy" or "men can't be trusted" are like pesky flies buzzing around inside of our heads. We can try a million different ways to fight them, but they'll probably keep coming back. Buddha discovered that the best way to deal with them is to sit and quietly acknowledge that these thoughts, as overwhelming as they seem, don't actually have power over us. We may not be able to stop them from whizzing around in our minds, but we *can* control our emotional and physical reactions to them. Like flies, they come and go, are never still, and can have a negative effect on our actions only if we allow them to. As human beings, we can expect that doubt, fear, jealousy, envy, greed, and hatred will come buzzing, especially when love is at stake. When we sense these emotions that Buddhists refer to as "poisons" or "hindrances to happiness," we should attempt to be as patient as possible and consider what caused them to arise in the first place. Only then can we make wise decisions about whether they're worth acting on or just pesky illusions that we should put out of our mind the way we would shoo a fly out of an open window.

• • • • • • •

Mini-Meditation: Forgive the Slimeball in Your Life

Bitter breakups and bad experiences can leave us with negative relationship baggage that we'd be much happier without. As hard as it is, the only way to let go of anger or resentment is to forgive the person or people who caused it. By forgiving someone, we remove unnecessary pain from our own hearts and create more space for love and happiness. It's not enough to just say "I forgive him" once and consider it done. We have to train our minds to let go of the nasty emotions. Try using this Buddhist forgiveness meditation to check your baggage for good:

Every day for a week (or longer, if necessary), picture the person in your mind and send him the message that you've forgiven him. Imagine your forgiveness filling him like soft, golden light. Imagine that forgiving him is instantly making your heart lighter and fuller. Remember that he is no longer the person that he used to be. Like you, he's changed. Continuing to be angry at a person who no longer exists is pointless. Extend your forgiveness out to him as an act of pure kindness, and hope that he has found the strength and wisdom to become a better person.

TRUTH AND DARES

Attempting to decode male behavior might be a favorite female pastime, but assuming that you can know what's going on in a guy's mind will leave both you and your beau feeling frustrated and misunderstood. It's hard enough to grasp the meaning behind our own actions, let alone intuit someone else's. To find out how a guy feels about you, the relationship, or anything else that you want to know, it's better to do the straightforward, incredibly gutsy thing, and *ask*. But first, do something even gutsier and preface the question by letting him know what your answer to the same question would be. By wearing our heart on our sleeves, we're taking a huge risk, and encouraging the guy we're dating to do the same. Whether his response is good news or bad news, being aware of the reality of a situation is always better than letting ourselves live in a fantasy world that will never deliver true happiness.

Another truth about love I've learned from Buddhism and tried to put into practice is that compassionate listening is the secret to getting truly close to someone. You may not realize it, but every time a guy dares to tell you something less than wonderful about himself—anything at all, from the dumbest detail to the most profound confession—whether you respond positively and with compassion directly effects how honest and open he'll be with you in the future. Let's say a new boyfriend were to inform you that he once spent a year in jail. If your first response is something that shows empathy, like "That must have been horrible, what was it like?" you're letting him know that you're there to find out more about who he is, not to judge him. Suddenly, there's one more ounce of trust and comfort between you. If you say something like "God, you must have done something *awful*," you're essentially punishing him for spilling his guts. Like when you rub a dog's nose in his business, he learns not to do it again.

When you think about it, the people that we're closest to in life are the ones who we feel we can tell anything to with the confidence that we'll get a supportive, loving response. And that doesn't mean it has to be an ass-kissing response. When our best friends disagree with our views, or think we're making a bad decision, they first do their best to see where we're coming from before giving us their opposing two cents. That initial empathy and benefit-of-the-doubt is the foundation of trust and intimacy. It's not a guarantee that you'll fall in love or stay in love forever, but it will allow you to actually get to know who it is you're dating.

The Eightfold Path to Recognizing a Good Guy

Ask yourself the following questions about the guy you're dating to see if he's helping you live the happiest life possible. Every "yes" is a vote in his favor. Every "no" is a clue that he might not be quite as wonderful as you deserve.

1. **Right Understanding:** Does he think things through instead of jumping to conclusions?
2. **Right Intentions:** Does he have positive goals for the future?
3. **Right Speech:** Does he talk to you honestly and openly about his feelings?
4. **Right Action:** Does he avoid doing things that go against his ethics?
5. **Right Livelihood:** Does he do his job to the best of his ability?
6. **Right Effort:** Does he finish what he starts?
7. **Right Mindfulness:** Is he thoughtful and reflective?
8. **Right Concentration:** Is he able to pay attention to the little details of life, while also keeping the bigger picture in mind?

HAPPILY EVER AFTER . . .
WITH A BUDDHIST TWIST

Buddhist philosophy applies to romance surprisingly well, considering that anyone seeking to reach a state of nirvana—free from all attachments and desires—would have absolutely no use for dating tips. You might think that a Buddhist version of love would involve not being attached to your lover at all—to be happy when he's around, and equally happy when he's not. Close, but that's actually a little more extreme than Buddha suggested. Being happy without your significant other is important, but there's nothing wrong with preferring his or her company to others or to being alone. Buddha's advice to non-monks that the "middle way" is the wisest applies here as it does to all other aspects of life. Just as we shouldn't eat, work, or sleep too much or too little, we also shouldn't focus on our romantic relationships too much or too little. As lovers we should be devoted, but still retain some independence; try to make our partner happy, but not over-sacrifice for his sake; enjoy his company, affection, and support, but never take advantage. In other words, the ideal Buddhist love is one that remains in balance.

The most relationship-friendly tenets of Buddhism address three truths that we often lose sight of as we get wrapped up in the momentum and rituals of pairing up and settling down.

1. **The most important time in your relationship is now.**
    Planning or just thinking about the future of a relationship is healthy once in a while, but not if it comes at the expense of experiencing the present moment. Enjoying our boyfriend's company and getting to know him should be our first two priorities in the here and now. Because if being together stops being fun or rewarding there may not be a future. It's comforting to prepare wisely for the months and years ahead, when it comes to our own finances, major events, or travel plans. But staying open and flexible to what life and love may surprise us with in the short term will make us far happier than crating a rigid emotional schedule that we may not be able—or even want to—follow.

It is by living a life in common with a person that we learn of that person's moral character; and then only if having insight ourselves, we have watched the person a long time.

It is only in conversations with a person that we learn of that person's wisdom and clarity of heart; and then only if, having insight ourselves, we have paid attention for a long time.

It is during times of trouble that we learn of another's fortitude; and then only if, having insight ourselves, we have paid careful attention for a long time.

2. Your feelings for each other will change—constantly.
At the highpoints of our love lives, when we feel like Nicole Kidman and Jude Law in their single *Cold Mountain* love scene, we naturally want things to stay that way for as long as possible. But, like any other emotions, the ones associated with love are bound to change from situation to situation and moment to moment. Don't worry—that doesn't mean that they can't always remain as strong. In a relationship we play many more roles for our partner than we may be aware of: sometimes we're maternal, productive, and pampering; sometimes we're the one who is being babied; sometimes we play the role of a best friend; other times our role is purely sexual. Each time there's a change in the way we interact, our feelings change as well. Think of your relationship as something dynamic and unpredictable. Let love happen to you.

3. You are responsible for your own happiness.

There's no doubt that romantic relationships can add to our overall happiness and sense of fun and fulfillment. That's why we pursue them in the first place. Still, our primary source of peace must come from inside ourselves, otherwise we'll never feel truly satisfied or confident. To bring the most to a relationship, we have to be able to live without it, and that requires taking time to take care of ourselves and enjoy the world on our own terms. Spending time one-on-one with friends and family members is necessary to maintaining our identities outside of a relationship, as is doing things completely alone. Our relationship with ourselves is really the one most essential to our happiness. Knowing and loving ourselves well will provide a foundation for every other happiness in our lives.

Monks Gone Wild: A Monk in Love

The terrible war flower
has left her footprints—
countless petals of separation and death
in white and violet.
Very tenderly, the wound opens itself in the depths
of my heart.
Its color is the color of blood,
its nature the nature of separation.

—Excerpted from "The Beauty of Spring Blocks My Way,"
by Thich Nhat Hanh

When he was a twenty-five, Thich Nhat Hanh, a Vietnamese Buddhist monk, poet, author, and Nobel Peace Prize nominee, fell in love with a twenty-year-old nun. It was New Year's Eve and they were on retreat together at a temple in a beautiful highland village. She returned his love, but they decided to let each other go in order to continue upholding their vows. He wrote "The Beauty of Spring Blocks My Way" less than twelve hours after making that heartbreaking decision, proving that monks can fall in love as hard and fast as any of us.

These days, you can get lectures by the Dalai Lama as well as Western scholars on DVD, which do a wonderful job of explaining the nuances of Buddhist philosophy—but good luck getting a friend to watch them with you. Because, well, let's just say they're a little dry. If it's movie night and you want to sneak a little Buddhist enlightenment into the mix, rent one of these:

Phörpa, *aka* The Cup *(1999)*

If you see one movie about Buddhism, it should probably be this one. *The Cup* is the first feature film made in the Himalayan kingdom of Bhutan and the first to be filmed in the Tibetan language by a Tibetan lama. In an isolated monastery a group of soccer-loving young monks are desperate to watch the '98 World Cup, but their teachers insist that attachment to such silliness would only interfere with their learning and meditation. The boys set about trying to trick their elders and rent a television so they can watch the match. Based on a true story, it very lightly portrays the difficulty of maintaining a Buddhist perspective in a changing world. Very funny. Very sweet.

Kundun *(1997)*

Director Martin Scorsese's poetic biography of the current Dalai Lama is a dramatic visual experience and an obvious ode to the beauty and serenity of Tibetan Buddhist culture. The sweeping views of stark mountain landscapes and ornate red-and-gold temples paired with a moving score by Philip Glass will either leave you deeply moved and inspired or very, very sleepy, depending on your appetite for action. During the film, excerpts from Buddhist texts are read, and the process by which the Dalai Lama is discovered as a child is shown in rich detail, as is his struggle with the decision to leave Tibet as the Chinese begin to invade and mercilessly slaughter thousands of his people. About the title: the Tibetans call the Dalai Lama *"Kundun,"* which means "the Presence."

Little Buddha *(1993)*

When a Buddhist lama dies, his devoted student heads out into the world in search of his teacher's reincarnated soul. He ends up in Seattle, and believes that his lama's spirit might be found in little Jesse Conrad (he finds two other candidates as well, and puts the children through a series of tests to discover who is really his reborn teacher). While telling the story of the interaction between the monk, Jesse, and Jesse's parents (played by Bridget Fonda and Chris Isaak), the movie simultaneously tells a version of Siddhartha Gautama's transformation into the Buddha (played by Keanu Reeves) that closely resembles the storyline of the novel *Siddhartha* written by Herman Hesse. This movie was directed by Bernardo Bertolucci, who is famous for his films *The Last Emperor* and *The Sheltering Sky*, and is based on a true story about a real Tibetan lama. The shots of India and Bhutan are absolutely gorgeous, and as a introduction to Buddha's discovery of the true nature of suffering, it's not bad—if you can handle Keanu's horrible attempt at an Indian accent.

Seven Years in Tibet *(1997)*

Also based on a true story, this is the tale of Heinrich Harrer (played by Brad Pitt), a Nazi-sympathizing Austrian mountain climber, who sets out to climb the Himalayas in an attempt to raise German morale. During the excursion, he and a companion are captured by the British army and interned in a POW camp. After escaping, Harrer sneaks into the holy Tibetan city of Lhasa in which he eventually meets and befriends the young

Dalai Lama. We get a limited but somewhat insightful view of the Dalai Lama's life and the Chinese occupation of Tibet through Harrer's eyes, but the story really revolves around Harrer's spiritual growth and realization of the pointlessness of war and violence. Brad Pitt puts in a solid performance. *Seven Years in Tibet* won't wow you, but it's definitely worth renting on a Sunday night.

6

Buddhist Secrets to Soulful Sex

I'm not sure if Buddha knew he was doling out the best sex advice of all time when he encouraged people to stay in the moment, clear their minds, and be aware of every sensation as it arises, but taking those principles straight to bed is a sure way to get more pleasure and satisfaction out of everything from a goodnight kiss to a toe-curling orgasm. Of all your less-than-satisfying sexual experiences, I bet that more often than not you were too stuck in your head to enjoy what was happening in your body. (The rest of the time it was probably because your partner didn't know what he was doing, but I'll get to that later.) Whether we're worrying about what our butt looks like, stressing over the status of the relationship, or preoccupied with a project we failed to finish at work that day, a buzzing, distracted brain makes deep, intense pleasure impossible. And if we're not fully present mentally and emotionally, we can't connect with our partner in a meaningful way. Great sex requires that we actually *be there*, physically and mentally, in the first place.

It also requires clear understanding—both of our own reasons for wanting sex and of the nature of sex itself. Ideally, sex is a sensual pleasure that we seek because it feels good, it satisfies one of our natural urges, and it symbolizes a romantic connection with a person we care about and are attracted to. If those were the only reasons for which we ever chose to sleep with someone (aside from wanting a baby, of course), life would be a lot less complicated, and sex would be amazing more of the time. Unfortunately we often hope sex will do things that it can't, like improve our self-esteem, strengthen a rocky relationship, or give us a sense of security. As with food, if we try to get more out of sex than is in its nature to provide, we end up suffering more.

Is That a Lingam in Your Pocket?

The Sanskrit word for vagina is *"yoni,"*
which means "sacred place."
A penis is called a *"lingam,"* or "lightning rod."

Thinking straight when you're horny isn't easy, but is necessary to ensure that we aren't getting into a frustrating or disappointing situation. It takes only a second to remind ourselves that sex is about physical pleasure and sharing our energy and passion with someone. If that's not what we're there to do, then it's time to put on the brakes and save ourselves some unhappiness. When we do have sex for the right reasons, it's our full awareness of what we are doing and the honest sharing of energy and passion that results in an experience that sends shivers up our spine. The more energy and passion we put out, the more thrilling sex will be.

FIVE STEPS TO NOOKIE NIRVANA

Making our sex lives more exciting and emotionally gratifying takes conscious effort and the courage to push past our own boundaries. Superficial enhancers such as lingerie and candles may increase the heat on a single night, but they won't inspire profound, long-term change. Focus on the following five goals and you'll not only orgasm more frequently, you'll begin to see a noticeable improvement in the intensity and intimacy of your sex life.

1. Create a sacred, sensual place. Transforming your bedroom into a haven of relaxation and positive energy can do a lot to separate sex from all of the stress that goes on in your life. Start by keeping the area around the bed clean, uncluttered, and completely free of anything that reminds you of work or other obligations. There should be no desk, no phone, no computer, and no television. But more importantly, make an agreement with your partner never to say anything angry, critical, or frustrating, or have any other kind of stressful conversation in the bedroom. Declare it a bitch-free zone where you relate to each other only as compassionate lovers, not as two people with busy schedules, bills to pay, and problems to solve. When you walk into your bedroom, you should feel yourself instantly breathing a sigh of relief to be in a place that's dedicated solely to pleasure and rest.

2. Be honest. Honesty in bed is everything. Without it there can be no intimacy, no real understanding, no deep satisfaction. All the reasons we have for not telling our partner how we feel or what we want—because we're afraid to hurt his feelings, we're embarrassed, we don't want to seem needy or difficult—pale in comparison to what we have to gain by opening up and expressing our desires, explaining our bodies, and sharing our emotions. If that isn't something you and your partner do on a regular basis, don't feel bad. Few couples do. But if you don't start somewhere it'll never happen, so say something true and daring about how you want to be turned on or touched. Clue him in to what he does that excites you and what you wish he would do more often (touch and kiss different parts of your body, rub your *yoni* with all of his fingers pressed together, whisper naughty things in your ear, anything and everything). Then ask him what *he* likes and wants. Being honest with your lover is the most powerful aphrodisiac there is. He may be incredibly good at intuiting what you want, but nothing is as effective as letting him know exactly how to please you, and letting you know how to please him. Also, if you fake orgasms, you absolutely must stop. It's a lie that does damage to your own self-esteem (you deserve the real thing!) and your sexual relationship. Admit that orgasm is difficult for you and ask him to help you get there. Remember: the more you expose yourself, the more intimacy there is to gain.

Monks Gone Wild:
The Wild Nights of Crazy Wisdom

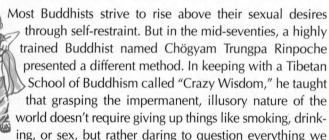

Most Buddhists strive to rise above their sexual desires through self-restraint. But in the mid-seventies, a highly trained Buddhist named Chögyam Trungpa Rinpoche presented a different method. In keeping with a Tibetan School of Buddhism called "Crazy Wisdom," he taught that grasping the impermanent, illusory nature of the world doesn't require giving up things like smoking, drinking, or sex, but rather daring to question everything we know—including our sexual ethics. Hundreds of hippies, including the beat poet Allen Ginsberg, flocked to Trungpa Rinpoche's retreats, and as they tried to abandon their moral attachments, many ended up drunk and naked. Trungpa Rinpoche himself slept with many of his female students and was criticized for taking advantage of his power. But Trungpa Rinpoche's teachings about sex comprised only a small if scandalous part of his legacy. He founded the Naropa Institute, the first Buddhist-inspired college in the West, as well as more than one hundred meditation centers around the world; wrote fourteen books on Buddhism, poetry, and art; and is often credited as the first person to make Buddhism accessible to Westerners.

3. Breathe into your body. If you find yourself feeling distracted or disconnected from your body in bed, try breathing deeply into the areas of your body that are being kissed, touched, or entered. Imagine the oxygen you pull in through your nose traveling to your breasts or *yoni* or wherever your lover is lavishing attention. Imagine that the oxygen is making your skin more sensitive, your body more responsive. When you feel your mind wandering, bring it back to the point at which your bodies are making contact and focus your breath and attention just there and nowhere else. Let the sensations take over your mind, let them be all that you think or care about. Allow yourself to do nothing but feel. When you're touching your partner, breathe deeply and focus on where your hands, lips, and/or other body parts are pressing against his body. Let those points of contact be the center of your universe.

4. Keep your eyes and ears open. Being fully aware of your partner's body is just as important as being aware of your own. During sex you can listen to his breathing and watch and feel his body move to discover what relaxes him, what excites him, and what brings him closest to orgasm. While lounging in bed, explore his body in a sensual way, inch by inch with your eyes and hands. From that point on, there's nothing to hide, nothing to be shy about. There's a kind of confidence and comfort that comes from knowing that your partner has seen and touched every part of you. Tell him everything that you love about his body as you lovingly kiss, feel, and gaze at him from head to toe. Encourage him to give you the same treatment. Most men would love to have complete access to their partner's body, they just don't know how to ask for the privilege.

5. Let go. With all the things we do to protect ourselves from being hurt, letting go and being vulnerable in bed can be a struggle. We're used to being self-conscious, to making sure that we're doing the right thing at the right time, to staying in control. But when it comes to orgasm, we have to kick all of those habits and completely let go. It's like getting so drunk that you can dance for hours and never worry for a minute that you look like MC Hammer. In becoming intoxicated by sexual energy, we can reach that same place of freedom and pleasure where we're able to move our bodies in whatever way feels best without caring what we look like or monitoring the sounds that are coming out of our mouths or trying to control the expressions on our faces. The only way to make that happen is to stop self-critical, self-conscious thoughts in their tracks and let them disappear. Refuse to allow yourself to think as you get more and more lost in what you're feeling. When words pop up in your mind (other than stuff along the lines of "Yes! Oh my god!") try to immediately drown them out with erotic sensations. Don't think, just feel, move, enjoy. Let go of everything that's holding you back until you feel like you're about to explode—it will be the best feeling you've had in your life.

· · · · · · ·

Mini Meditation: Feel the Rapture

The sensation of the lingam first sliding into the yoni is one of the most pleasurable and satisfying moments of sex, and it's one worth contemplating for a few blissful moments before letting the action continue. The next time you have sex, ask your partner to stop as soon as he's entered you and tell him that you want to take some time to revel in the feeling of having him inside you. Lie very still and con-

sider the very real, physical connection that's taking place. Appreciate how crazy sex is, how strange, how wonderful. Remind yourself how lucky you are to be engaged in one of the most pleasurable activities on the planet. Determine to make the most of every second.

TANTRIC TRICKS FOR CREATING
A DEEP CONNECTION

The most basic Buddhist teachings about sex express two simple ideas. The first is that trying to achieve happiness through sex is a hopeless cause because, like hunger, lust can never be satisfied (we can have sex a thousand times and still want more). The second is that people should show compassion for themselves and others by avoiding sex that is illegal or harmful. That's pretty much it. But as Buddha's teachings merged with other religions and traditions in India, China, and Nepal, something called Tantra began to develop. The origins of Tantra are difficult to trace. There is a legend that Buddha once taught a king how to reach nirvana by using his sexual energy. As the story goes, these teachings were then passed along in secrecy from one generation of royalty to the next until they were eventually written down and made available to the general public.

Regardless of where and how it began, modern day Tantric Buddhism as it is practiced in Tibet is a highly mystical and ceremonial form of Buddhism in which practitioners attempt to reach enlightenment with the aid of things such as ritual hand movements, symbols, prayer, and chanting. Sex plays a very small and mostly symbolic role, and the goal is to control sexual energy, not indulge it. In India, a form of Tantra did arise that focused directly on sex and the body, but the goal was still spiritual enlightenment, not physical satisfaction. Long story short, the concept of Tantric Sex that has been reborn in the West has very little to do with either Indian or Tibetan Tantra, and while it does incorporate some basic principals of Buddha's philosophy, it's more of a mishmash of ideas collected from many different sources. Even so, Western Tantra has undeniably produced some helpful ways of feeling closer to your lover. The following three Tantric techniques have been endorsed by modern day sex therapists because they really do work.

Eye-Gazing

Looking our partner directly in the eyes can sometimes feel awkward and a little too intense, but it's something worth doing more often and for longer periods of time. By gazing directly at your partner, you let him know that you're completely focused on him and nothing else. You express that you're interested in what he's feeling, what he's thinking, who he is. You make yourself vulnerable by letting him see the emotion in your own eyes. You force yourself to confront any fears you might have about your relationship. As you look into his eyes, register any feelings of embarrassment, love, attraction, fear, or anything else that might come up, but try not to look away. The more willing you both are to acknowledge and accept how it feels, the closer and more bonded you'll become. You might even want to suggest a night when you have sex while maintaining eye-contact the entire time. While you're doing it, it may feel like an absolutely ridiculous exercise, but when it's over, you'll know each other a little—or a lot—better than before.

Thousands of candles can be lighted from a single candle, and the life of the candle will not be shortened. Happiness never decreases by being shared.

Taking Turns

You probably already fall into a pattern of sex in which one person lays back and the other takes the lead. The perk is that it allows the one being pampered to fully enjoy the experience without having to perform at the same time. But it's crucial that you each spend as much time receiving pleasure as you do giving it. It doesn't matter if you give and take the same amount on the same night or not, but overall, from week to week and month to month, you should both feel equally lavished with attention. When we make our partner's pleasure the priority, we're honoring him, respecting him, appreciating him, devoting ourselves to him. It sends the message that we value him in our lives and want to make him happy. If you feel that you give more TLC in bed than you get, don't demand more, but do request that you each take a night to pamper your partner completely. Then explain to him what "being pampered" means to you in specific terms, and find out what it means to him.

Massage and Bathing

As good as sex feels, sometimes being babied feels even better. And no matter how big or masculine the guy you're dating is, he no doubt loves having his neck and shoulders massaged, his feet rubbed, and his hair washed in the shower. Similar to the way our parents cared for us as kids, this kind of sweet, loving touch can create as many feelings of security, comfort, and closeness as the most passionate sex. Get into a habit of massaging each other while watching movies on the couch; taking baths together and scrubbing each other's backs; and running you fingers through each other's hair just because it feels good.

Play Time

Doing something neither of you have ever done before is an exhilarating way to bond, in bed and out. Depending on how experienced one or both of you are, that may be as easy as having sex in a tent in your backyard, busting out a can of whipped cream, or taking turns talking dirty. But even if you've been around the block and back again, there are plenty of imaginative sex positions and toys out there still to discover. Bring your laptop to bed and browse sites like www.goodvibes .com, www.babeland.com, or www.blowfish.com to find tempting toys. And consider getting a copy of an updated *Kama Sutra*—the ancient Indian guide to lovemaking that includes dozens of creative sexual positions—for your bedside table. By breaking new ground together, you build trust and give each other crucial room to grow and change sexually.

ULTRA-PASSION POSITIONS

Any sexual configuration can be romantic and intense, but the most romantic of all tend to be those in which a couple can see each other's faces and bodies, and/or feel the greatest amount of full-body contact. Both inspire a sense of total openness and deep intimacy. Add the following to your repertoire if they're not already on your list of favorites.

The Sacred Embrace

Sit in your partner's lap, wrap your legs around his waist and your arms around his neck, as he wraps his arms around your hips. Thrusting in this position should be slow and rhythmic as you simultaneously kiss each other's mouths and necks. In Tantra, this position symbolizes the blissful union of wisdom and compassion.

Eyes Wide Open

As you lie with pillows under your back to raise your head and torso to a forty-five-degree angle, your partner should lie between your legs and support himself with his arms. In this position you can both look down and see the erotic sight of his *lingam* entering your *yoni*. And your mouths are always within kissing range.

Blanket Love

These three very similar positions deliver the most skin-on-skin contact possible:

1. Have your partner lie on his back and then straddle him so that his *lingam* is deep in your *yoni*. Then lean slowly forward as you swing your legs so that they rest directly on top of his. Make small up and down movements with your hips to create friction.

2. Lie on your stomach as your partner enters you from behind, resting his torso on top of yours. He can kiss your neck and shoulders and reach his hands under your abdomen to rub your clitoris.

3. If your partner has a longer than average *lingam*, lie on your back and have him enter you and lie down so that his torso is pressed against your chest. He should then swing his legs so that they rest on top of yours or on either side of yours. Controlled thrusting will create incredible, intense sensations for both of you.

Slow Him Down

Also swiped from Tantra, these moves can keep a speedy lover from finishing too quickly.

Pull Here—Wrapping your thumb and forefinger around his scrotum just above his testicles and gently tugging downward can help delay orgasm.

Give It a Squeeze—Firmly squeezing the head of the *lingam* reduces sensitivity, helping to dial back his excitement a few notches.

Stop and Start—When you sense your partner getting close to his peak, stop touching his *lingam* in any way, lie by his side, and spend a few minutes kissing until his *lingam* loses some of its hardness. Slowly resume contact until he again comes close to orgasm and then stop again. Repeat one more time, before continuing sex until he comes. This technique gives you more time to get aroused, especially if he uses the breaks to manually or orally stimulate your *yoni*.

~ Dharma Groupies ~

These high-profile groups have helped to make Buddha's smiling face a pop-culture icon of personal freedom and world peace. Anti-establishment types who are looking for a more open-minded, tolerant, satisfying way to live seem to naturally seek out Buddhism. They also seem to seek out sex, drugs, and rock 'n' roll. But, contrary to popular belief, the two aren't actually related.

1950s, The Beats: Jack Kerouac, Gary Snyder, Allen Ginsberg, and many other beats were drawn to Buddhism in part because of its focus on the here and now. Both Buddhism and Beat Poetry emphasize the significance of staying connected to the present moment, no matter how mundane it may get. The two also share an appreciation for what you can learn about yourself and life in general from paying attention to your thoughts as they arise (Buddhists meditate, Beats use free-association). Kerouac was clearly inspired and challenged by what he read about Buddhist philosophy, but never became a practicing Buddhist in any traditional sense. Ginsberg, who did practice, wrote the following in the Fall 1992 issue of *Tricycle:*

> "[Kerouac] introduced me to [Buddhism] in the form of letters reminding me that suffering was the basis of existence, which is the first Noble Truth in Buddhism. I was at the time a more or less left-wing liberal progressive intellectual, and I was insulted that Kerouac was telling me that the real basis of existence was suffering. I thought this was a personal insult and didn't realize that he was simply telling me what he had realized was the basic nature of life."

The Beats weren't the first American writers to praise Buddha. Henry David Thoreau gave him props back in the nineteenth century. But the Beats were definitely the first to make Buddhism cool.

1970s, The Hippies: After experimenting with sex and drugs only to discover that neither provided lasting satisfaction, many tie-dye-wearing members of the Hippie movement turned to Eastern philosophy as a far wiser and healthier path toward peace and openness. The Vietnam War had shown them firsthand what the results of intolerance and lack of regard for human life could lead to, and Buddhism's central tenets of compassion and nonviolence provided a soothing refuge. But it was also a demanding one. On one hand, the Buddhist concept of universal connectedness fit right in with the "We're all brothers and sisters" mantra that hippies were already trying to live by. On the other, the self-discipline required to be a formal Buddhist is a far cry from free love and LSD. But those who were serious about it formed new Buddhist communities (often led by a Western man or woman) and began to develop practices that revolved around meditation. Some of these communities took on the traditions of well-established Asian schools, while others veered in new, different, and sometimes highly controversial directions. (See Crazy Wisdom, page 104.)

1990s, The Rock Stars: In 1996, the Beastie Boys' Adam Yauch, himself an aspiring Buddhist since first hearing the Dalai Lama speak, organized a benefit concert in San Francisco's Golden Gate Park to raise money to help "Free Tibet." With bands and musicians including Björk, the Smashing Pumpkins, Sonic Youth, A Tribe Called Quest, and the Fugees on the roster, the concert generated a huge amount of publicity and made most of Generation X suddenly aware of the plight of this oppressed country and its ancient and now exiled religion. "The bodhisattva vow [a formal promise to follow the eightfold path] is something that I had taken to myself, a bunch of years before I had read about it in Buddhism," said Yauch while being interviewed by the Buddhist magazine *Shambhala Sun.* "And then when I started learning about it in Buddhism, I thought, 'Yeah . . . that makes sense.'" As millions of fans rocked out, the message that Buddhism was something wonderful and sacred and needed to be preserved was being broadcast loud and clear.

2000s, The Hipsters: Kickstarted by the huge resurgence of yoga, tai chi, and other Eastern forms of exercise in the United States, the new Buddha Groupies are smart, slightly rebellious, happiness-seeking humanitarians in their twenties and thirties who are looking for spirituality without righteousness, and peace of mind without illusions. Images of Buddha are showing up on tank tops, coffee cups, bags, wallets, and just about everything else. Even the number of Buddha tattoos seems to be on the rise. By hand picking the teachings and traditions that best apply to their lives from a variety of different schools, many of these aspiring Buddhists are helping to define what the new Western Buddhism will someday look like. No doubt the global visibility of the sixteenth Dalai Lama, the spiritual and political leader of Tibet, has played a major part in drumming up curiosity about the ancient philosophy. He looks as joyful and serene as any statue of Buddha. Not even Nike could come up with a better ad campaign than that.

7

Blissful Body,
Open Mind

Take a minute to think about those times when you've felt completely blissful. What experiences come to mind? Maybe it's a ninety-minute rubdown from a massage therapist who truly understands the human body; a long soak in a warm, lavender-scented bath; slow, intense sex with someone you love; or swimming in a cool, clean lake on a hot day. If you're an athlete it might be that intense pleasure zone you hit when you stop thinking about the fact that you're running or shooting a basket or riding a wave, feeling instead as if your head were floating gloriously a few inches above your shoulders.

All of the above create a state of mind in which existence feels easy. We're completely engaged in the moment. There's no struggle, no thoughts, no discomfort, no desire to be anywhere else, no desire at all—we're just *there*, feeling the high, and it's absolutely amazing. In these moments, the boundaries between ourselves and the world begin to dissolve, and there's a sense of being part of something bigger and more meaningful. You feel inherently connected to everything and yet completely free at the same time. Your mind feels expansive and open. Everything outside of the present moment suddenly doesn't matter as much. When you're in the midst of an orgasm, when you're effortlessly gliding down a powdery slope on a snowboard, when you're lying on the beach feeling the sun warm your skin, or when you're standing on top of a mountain, you don't care what your name is, where you live, whether you like your job, or if you have enough money in the bank. You move beyond the mundane level of reality and into one that feels deeper, more infinite, and more gratifying.

These kinds of experiences don't happen every day. But they do happen. And as hard as they are to describe and analyze, peak experiences can teach us a lot about what it means to be happy from head to toe.

. . . .

Mini-Meditation: Remind Yourself That You Rock

Apparently low self-esteem was as rampant around 470 BC as it is now. Noticing how much unhappiness was caused by self-criticism, Buddha gave his students the following tip: "You can search throughout the entire universe for someone who is more deserving of your love and affection than you are yourself, and that person is not to be found anywhere. You, yourself, as much as anybody in the entire universe, deserve your love and affection." Being compassionate toward ourselves isn't always easy. We have a habit of overlooking our best attributes and only paying attention to the ways in which we're less than perfect. Loving-kindness meditation helps to rebuild self-esteem and remind ourselves that we deserve TLC as much as anyone else. The next time you're being hard on yourself, draw a bath, climb in, and when you begin to relax, repeat the following five times:

"May I be well and happy. May I be peaceful and calm. May my mind be free from envy, anger, and sadness. May I be content. May my heart be filled with love."

OPEN UP AND SAY AHHHH . . .

Other than sex, which I discussed at length in the previous chapter, the most blissful physical activities that come to my mind are, in no specific order: being in the midst of breathtakingly gorgeous nature; getting a deep-tissue massage; and finishing a long, challenging yoga class. When doing any of these things, I've noticed that the same thought pattern usually occurs, which you might be able to relate to. Using a Swedish massage as an example, here's how my mind slowly transforms from stressed-out to blissed-out:

STAGE ONE: *Total monkey mind*

When the massage therapist first starts kneading my back I'm usually completely unable to enjoy it in spite of the fact that the pressure of her hands feels undeniably good. My mind is jumping from topic to topic like a monkey swinging from branch to branch. I keep up a ridiculous mental dialogue, along the lines of *Wow, this is great. This is the good life. I should really be extremely happy at this moment. I wonder if I remembered to shut off my cell phone. This massage therapist is the best, I should tell Alli to book an appointment with her. Hmmm, I wonder what Alli is doing right now . . . why am I wondering what she's doing when I'm here getting this awesome massage? If only I could stop thinking about how blissful this is, I could actually be blissful. But I can't stop thinking!* I'm so self-conscious about the fact that something good is going down that I can't even enjoy it while it's happening. When we're stuck in our own heads it's because we're focusing inwardly, on our opinions, concerns, worries, pasts, futures, friends, job, etc., rather than paying attention to what we're currently experiencing through our five senses. Our mind is just a crazy, out of control little monkey.

STAGE TWO: *Mind melts into body*

After breathing deeply and making an effort to quiet my mind and settle into my skin, I eventually stop thinking so much and start enjoying the sensation of tension being worked out of my muscles. My body starts to warm up and relax. I can smell the scented oil in the air and hear the shuffle of the therapist's feet around the massage table. My thoughts get fewer and farther between as intense feelings take over. Mind and body begin to meld together and feel deeply connected. The more I let go of any thoughts that wander beyond the present moment, the more my sense of pleasure grows.

STAGE THREE: *Mind and body begin to open*

In this last stage, which doesn't always happen, there's a kind of breakthrough where I feel completely in synch with every sensation, with my surroundings, and with the massage therapist as well. My mind is aware but very quiet and at ease. My body feels loose and relaxed. Some of the therapist's techniques are soothing, others are so intense they're extremely uncomfortable. In this state of heightened relaxation, I'm able to register both the comfort and the discomfort and just breathe with them. There's a feeling of peace—a sense of just being, without resistance or craving or tension of any kind. When playing sports, having sex, or anytime I'm fully engaged in a physical activity, there's also a sense of fearlessness. I'm so caught up in the moment, I don't worry about anything. It's at that point when all of these feelings come together that I experience a little bit of what I consider to be *bliss*.

Awakening is the recovery of that awesome freedom into which we were born but for which we have substituted the pseudo-independence of a separate self. No matter how much it frightens us, no matter how much we resist it, such freedom is right at hand. It may break into our lives at any time, whether we seek it or not, enabling us to glimpse a reality that is simultaneously more familiar and more elusive than anything we have ever known, in which we find ourselves both profoundly alone and profoundly connected to everything. Yet the force of habit is such that suddenly it is lost again and we are back to unambiguous reality.

—*Buddhism Without Beliefs* by Stephen Batchelor

Maybe the above descriptions are completely familiar to you. Maybe they're not. The next time you have a chance to indulge in physical pleasure, pay attention to your thoughts and feelings and do your best to be aware of what makes the most climactic moment of the experience so exceptionally good. Figure out for yourself what bliss is really made of.

The massage eventually ends, I go back out into the world, and that sense of comfort, openness, connection, and nonresistance begins to fade. But acknowledging the qualities of mind that exist during temporary bliss can teach us something very surprising and important about happiness.

What I've learned is that by trying to imitate what I think and feel during my brief brushes with bliss, I'm able to feel more content and satisfied no matter where I am or what I'm doing. When I find myself in a bad mood or a difficult situation, I remind myself to try and stay fully present in the moment, both mentally and physically, to remain open to whatever might happen next whether it makes me comfortable or uncomfortable, and to acknowledge that I am connected to everyone else around me—what I do affects them and what they do affects me. When I succeed in thinking this way, it always produces the happiest possible outcome under the circumstances. These states of mind—awareness, acceptance, compassion—are the same ones that Buddha suggested we cultivate during meditation. Which is one of the many reasons why Buddhism rings so true to me. The Buddhist concept of bliss perfectly fits my humble little encounters with it. Buddha taught that we don't need any outward stimulation to reach a state of deep contentment. "The mind," he said, "is the source of happiness and unhappiness." But things like massages, warm baths, and great workouts can remind us of how it feels to be in state of calm, open contentment when we haven't felt that way in a long time. They give us a point of reference and a goal. These reminders motivate us to want to achieve and maintain that state as often and as long as possible. The only way to do that is to learn how to create and maintain it ourselves from the inside out. This takes practice, practice, practice, whether you do it by sitting down and meditating or just keeping the concepts of awareness, openness, and compassion in mind as you go about your day. But while you're working on cooking up inner bliss, by all means go ahead and make that massage appointment.

BUDDHA + YOGA = BLISS + BEAUTY

Few yoga teachers ever mention the fact that in India, yoga isn't just a form of exercise, it's a complex religion in which the poses, or *asanas,* play only a tiny part. Yogic and Buddhist philosophy have a lot in common (when it comes to meditation and ethics, they're pretty much identical), but much of the yogic tradition involves the kind of mystical language that we skeptical Westerners have a hard time relating to. The result is that we learn all about the physical benefits of yoga but seldom hear about the ways that it can help us to get and stay happy.

By honing in on the harmony between Buddhist ideas and yogic *asanas*, it's possible to score a healthier, more blissful body and a calmer mind at the same time. Here's what they have in common and why experiencing them together can make our lives both in and out of the yoga studio sweeter and easier.

Awareness

If we're in the middle of a yoga pose and our mind wanders the slightest bit away from what we're doing, we start to wobble. We can't do the pose well if we don't at least focus most of our attention on it. The more focus we devote to carefully adjusting our body, the easier it is to move exactly the way we want to. Attention is what enables us to gain and maintain control—to get the results we want. Buddha taught that the same is true for every moment of our lives. The more present we are at any given moment, the more skillfully we're able to handle any given situation.

Balance

Every *asana* is designed to demonstrate the wisdom of living a balanced life. If we lean our torso to the left, we have to lean our hips to the right to avoid falling over. If we pull our weight forward with our arms we have to lean back to remain upright. In the same way, Buddha found that in order to experience the least amount of suffering and the largest amount of happiness, we should not sleep too much or too little, eat too much or too little, or work too much or too little. Keeping our lives in balance in every way—not over-indulging in our desires or denying ourselves what we need—is the only way to feel good in our skin.

Breathe

If we want to move further into a yoga pose we have to continue to breathe. The urge to stop breathing is the physical manifestation of our urge to prevent change. We want to hold a pose, to stay where we are, so we hold our breath. Soon the discomfort gets so bad that the posture falls apart. In yoga we have to continue to breathe in order to continue to progress. In life, we have to continue to accept constant change in order to be happy. Buddha discovered that resisting change only makes us more uncomfortable. Allowing our breath to move in and out parallels the way we should allow every moment to arise and pass without trying to stop it and keep everything just the way it is.

Release

The best moments in yoga occur when we're able to release some muscle tension, allowing our bodies to soften and become more flexible. It never feels like a matter of strength. It's more of a sudden melting, a lessening of resistance, a lessening of the fear that we won't be able to do it or that it will hurt, and when we finally let go it feels *sooooo* good. Similarly, Buddhism is all about seeking happiness through lessening our resistance to the way things are, letting go of the tension and fear inside of our heads and hearts, and allowing ourselves to become more flexible and open. Buddha taught that the happiest, most natural human state is one of total openness and no fear. By practicing both Buddhism and yoga, we work at slowly returning to that natural state of bliss.

Want a Better Body Image? Get Hot and Bothered

In the 1970s a yoga guru named Bikram Choudhury created a controversial class that takes place in a 100 to 115 degree room and consists of 26 specific postures that thoroughly work the entire body in 90 minutes. Why the crazy heat? Choudhury explains in his book *Bikram's Beginning Yoga Class:* "Suppose you are going to make a sword. You start with a piece of fine steel and the first thing you do is put the steel in the fire and heat it up. When the steel is hot, it becomes soft. Then you can hammer it and slowly you make it change shape to the sword you want. This is the natural way. Now if you don't heat it up and start hammering the cold steel, nothing is going to happen to the steel, but you'll break your hand, the hammer, your arm and all your connecting joints." The heat not only succeeds in making your body more malleable, it has the indirect effect of boosting body image. In Bikram class, everyone wears as little as possible to maximize the cooling effect of sweat evaporating off of their skin. So you end up surrounded by dozens of other half-naked people, all standing in front of a massive full-length mirror. There is always someone there with a fitter body than yours, and someone with a flabbier one. As you attempt the *asanas* one by one you see exactly what your body looks like and what it's capable of. After just a few weeks, you stop feeling so shy about the body that so many other people are seeing bend and stretch in full, sweat-drenched glory two or three times a week and start seeing it as a work in progress that you can be proud of. The heat also has the effect of forcing you to concentrate on your breathing much more than in any other yoga class because if you stop breathing, you'll probably pass out. Bikram yoga isn't for everyone, but if you can take the heat, the benefits can be huge.

Equanimity

For those of us who have done yoga before, we know that there are good yoga classes and not-so-good yoga classes. There are exhilarating moments and frustrating moments. Times when we want to run from the room and times when we wish we could do yoga all day long. But whether we're enjoying ourselves or inwardly groaning, we stick with it and finish class because we know that in the end we'll be happier if we just take the good with the bad. The Buddhist principle of equanimity—facing all things whether pleasant or unpleasant with a calm, even temper—encourages us to do the same in every situation. Don't constantly run from bad situations (unless you're in physical danger) and chase after good ones. Because, once again, both the bad and the good will continue to happen whether we like it or not. Try to hold your composure through thick and thin and you'll end up more satisfied with your life and yourself because you'll realize that you can handle anything.

Compassion

Good yoga teachers always remind their students that it doesn't matter how perfectly we do each posture, only that we try the right way. They emphasize that we should never force our bodies to go further than they can or we'll get injured. By following that advice, we learn to be gentle and compassionate with our bodies. To be sensitive to what it can and can't do at each moment in class. A Buddhist strives to be compassionate and forgiving, not only toward herself but also toward everyone else around her. On any given day, in any moment, we can and should do only our best and not expect anything more from ourselves or anyone else.

Doing yoga with Buddhist ideas in mind is an amazing way to improve our bodies and our overall well-being. The changes happen slowly but steadily. As every day of practice (which can be as laid-back as trying to see things from a Buddhist perspective and doing a few yoga poses ïonce a day or as intense as meditating every day and doing yoga three or four times a week) goes by we become a little more content, a little more tolerant, a little stronger, a little healthier, a little happier.

Monks Gone Wild: Kung Fu Masters

Around 540 AD an Indian Buddhist missionary— according to legend he was known as The Blue-Eyed Demon—visited the Shaolin or "new forest" temple in northern China, where he entered a cave and meditated for nine years before reaching enlightenment. When he left the cave he began to teach the monks of the temple there that sitting meditation (called "Chan" in Chinese and "Zen" in Japanese) was the best means to reaching nirvana. The only problem was that all of that sitting made the monks lethargic and unhealthy. So The Blue-Eyed Demon taught them a series of exercises that incorporated the Zen

principles of focused awareness and perfect balance. Over time those exercises developed into Shaolin kung fu. The Buddhist influence on kung fu created warriors who would never attack first and would fight only in self-defense; who never showed signs of pride or egotism; and whose minds had been made impervious to fear or weakness. The monks became a powerful fighting force—always devoted to just causes—until the introduction of firearms into China in the late nineteenth century made their skills irrelevant. The Shaolin temple began to fall apart. In the 1950s and '60s, the Chinese communist dictator Mao Tse-Tung outlawed kung fu and persecuted any remaining Shaolin monks. The original temple was revived in the late 1980s as the result of a sudden surge in popularity of martial arts films. Today, young boys—and a handful of girls—still go there to learn kung fu and Buddhism.

THE ZEN OF BODY IMAGE MAINTENANCE

In our culture, women's bodies are constantly being picked apart, praised and criticized, loved and hated, overindulged or starved, run down or underused. We're seldom kind to or forgiving of the body that carries us around all day. Which makes no sense considering how essential it is to our well-being. The sooner we can wake up and realize that taking care of and feeling good about our bodies isn't as hard as everyone makes it out to be, the sooner we'll achieve a higher level of happiness. There are three elements of Buddhist practice that I've found to be enormously inspiring when it comes to health and body image.

The first is the concept of what Buddha called the "middle path." He taught that "avoiding the extremes gives vision and knowledge and leads to calm, realization, enlightenment, and nirvana." The two extremes he was referring to were self-indulgence and self-mortification, aka having too much or too little of a good thing. Whether it's food, clothes, exercise, or even our opinion of ourselves, extremes lead straight to suffering. The truth of this is easy to prove. Eat too little and you suffer from hunger. Eat too much and you suffer from being too full. Worry too much about fashion and you shortchange other parts of your life. Worry too little about fashion and you could be judged unfairly by others. Exercise too much and you risk injury. Exercise too little and you risk illness. Think too highly of yourself and you'll lack compassion and humility. Think too little and you won't have the confidence to achieve your goals. To have just the right amount of a good thing is to be in balance and feel no suffering. Balance in all things should always be our goal.

The second helpful concept is that of mindfulness. It's impossible to achieve balance in our lives if we're not paying attention to when and where we're out of balance. Whether we're at dinner, shopping, or looking in the mirror, it's all too easy to not think clearly, to let our heads be filled with a whirlwind of negative and positive thoughts that leave us feeling confused about who we are and what we want and need. The very first lesson of Buddhism is STOP and CLEAR YOUR MIND, so that you can SEE STRAIGHT. It takes constant awareness to keep ourselves from falling out of balance. Achieving that awareness isn't complicated. All it takes, in any situation, is a PAUSE and a QUESTION. Step back and ask yourself: Will eating another bite make me feel better or worse? Will buying this dress really improve my life? Am I being unfair to my body by wanting it to look different from the way that it does, given my current lifestyle? Then answer yourself honestly. Once you have an answer, try to act in accordance with that answer. Of course, that's the hardest part. Often we know exactly what is in our best interest but don't have the willpower to do it. The remedy for lack of willpower is to try. Try today. Try tomorrow. Try again after that. You *will* get better and better at it. Trying = practice = improvement. You are bound to improve because it won't take long for you to realize that when you ask yourself what you really need to be happy, give yourself an honest answer, and then act accordingly, you end up happier than if you don't. Seeing the formula work over and over again will slowly transform those first few attempts to resist going to extremes into a habit of balance-seeking that feels perfectly natural.

The third concept has to do with the subjectivity of perception. The reason that Buddha concluded that happiness and unhappiness are all in the mind is because he discovered that whether something is good or bad is completely based on our ideas about that thing. To some people, lobster guts are a delicacy. To others, they're disgusting. Every time we open our eyes and look at a room, a person, a bowl full of Häagen Daaz, *we create that world.* If two women walk into a party, each will see a very different scene, depending on how their individual minds work. One woman, whose mind has been trained to judge other women and herself by appearance, might scan the room and start comparing other women's bodies and clothes to her own. Based on whether she feels inferior or superior to most of them, she will feel either pleased or threatened. The other woman may have very little interest in looks but prefer people who are counterculture. That woman will seek out people who voice opinions that go against the mainstream. If she can't find any, she'll think that the party sucks. Because the criteria for how we judge a situation or person is all in our minds, we have control over those criteria. We can change them. We can see differently if we want to. And for many of us, when it comes to our body image, it's crucial to our happiness that we learn to think and see differently.

Buddha began his search for enlightenment with the most basic logic. In order to stop being unhappy, we must identify what is making us unhappy, and then change it. With respect to body image, you probably already know the thoughts and actions that make you miserable. If you're like me, they include: comparing yourself to other women, looking at women's magazines that present images of ideal female figures that are emaciated, eating too much, standing in front of the mirror and criticizing the parts of your body that you don't like. Because I know that I have control over how I think and act, I've decided to try and stop doing these things. The effects of that simple decision have been nothing less than astounding.

- When I see a woman walking down the street and feel an urge to look at her, I check in with myself to find out what my motivation is. If it's to criticize her, compare her body to mine, or anything else negative, I give myself a mental slap on the wrist and either don't look at her at all or determine to look at her with compassion and friendliness. Sometimes I imagine that she is a friend of mine or my sister.

- I make a concerted effort *not* to flip through fashion magazines when I'm waiting for a haircut, sitting around at the doctor's office, or anywhere else, because I know that, while they might be fun and entertaining for some women, they make me feel inadequate. Maybe someday I'll have the peace of mind to observe all of that stuff without feeling the tiniest crack in my self-confidence, but until then it's certainly easy enough to read a book instead.
- As I'm eating, I stay aware of how my stomach feels. When I can tell it's reaching maximum capacity, I make a conscious decision to either keep eating because the food is so damn good that it's worth feeling stuffed for, or to stop because it's not worth it. Half of the time I realize that what I'm eating isn't even that good in the first place. And, I admit, a good 10 percent of the time I completely pig out.
- When I get out of the shower and pass a full-length mirror, I try to notice one thing I like about my body for every flaw that catches my eye. I also remind myself to be grateful for all the ways my body serves me well. Although it's hard to ignore the little wrinkles that keep popping up, I try not to take my health or youth for granted.

These techniques are my ways of feeling more satisfied with the body I have right now. I still have my fair share of self-critical, insecure days when I declare war on my extra-meaty thighs and glare at skanky bartenders, but they happen a lot less often than they used to. Paying attention to the beliefs, attitudes, and habits that make us less than kind to ourselves, and finding realistic ways to change them, is the simple, logical path to balance and happiness. Alas, it's something we have to work at one small step at a time—but the results are more than worth it.

~ Bunsen Buddha ~

"With the ever growing impact of science on our lives, religion and spirituality have a greater role to play in reminding us of our humanity. There is no contradiction between the two. Each gives us valuable insights into the other. Both science and the teachings of the Buddha tell us of the fundamental unity of all things."
—The Dalai Lama

One of the most mystical legends about Buddha describes how he popped out of his mother's womb and instantly started walking and talking. When Buddhism comes up in conversation, that's the kind of story that makes scientists—and most other people—shake their heads and politely excuse themselves from the room. But the very core teachings of Buddha—that meditation can help us to make sense of our emotions, reduce stress, and improve happiness—is something that has been seriously interesting Western scientists and academics for the past decade. As PhDs and MDs try meditation for themselves and, more importantly, conduct empirical studies on people who meditate on a regular basis, they're discovering that Buddha's methods have an unmistakably beneficial effect on the brain and the body.

At the University of Wisconsin's Laboratory for Affective Neuroscience, Tibetan monks have been hooked up to brain monitors and observed as they meditated into a deep state of calm. Lab director Richard Davidson, PhD, found that during meditation the area of a monk's brain associated with positive emotion lit up like a Christmas tree.[1]

Another study by Davidson and Jon Kabat-Zinn, PhD, founder of the Stress Reduction Clinic at the University of Mas-

[1] Daniel Goleman, *Destructive Emotions: A Scientific Dialogue with the Dalai Lama* (New York: Bantam Doubleday Dell, 2003).

sachusetts, proved that you don't have to be a monk to get that mental buzz. In 1997, they recruited a group of young employees at a small biotech company to begin meditating once a week for eight weeks. Those employees who stuck to the meditation practice showed increased activity in their brain's pleasure zone—a boost that was still present when they were tested again, four months later—and reported feeling more positive and at ease. Meditators who showed the greatest increase in brain activity also produced more disease-fighting antibodies, suggesting that meditation also strengthens the immune system.[2]

Many psychologists and major health institutions already prescribe meditation to their patients as an effective, drug-free way to improve their health and well-being. And more research is now underway. An organization called the Mind and Life Institute, based in Boulder, Colorado, has the sole purpose of bringing scientists and Buddhists together to gain a greater understanding of the human mind and the nature of reality. Every year it holds a conference that brings new findings about meditation to light. You can check out the latest discoveries at www.mindandlife.org.

---

[2]Richard J. Davidson, Jon Kabat-Zinn, Jessica Schumacher, Melissa Rosenkranz, Daniel Muller, Saki F. Santorelli, Ferris Urbanowski, Anne Harrington, Katherine Bonus, John F. Sheridan, "Alterations in Brain and Immune Function Produced by Mindfulness Meditation," *Psychosomatic Medicine,* 2003, 65, pp. 564–70.

8
Zen Escapes

One the most appealing aspects of Buddhism is that you don't need to buy anything or go anywhere to reap the benefits. Sure, it can help to go to a meditation class or attend a lecture or two, but you certainly don't have to. Buddha constantly reminded his students that there is only one tool necessary to achieving happiness and serenity, and that's a clear-thinking, open mind. But if your mind happens to be feeling a little dull around the edges and not quite as expansive as it could be, hitting the road is just what the guru ordered. Given that we can contemplate the nature of existence anywhere, there's no reason not to mull it over while hanging out on a beach in Mexico, sitting next to a fireplace in a log cabin, or soaking in a lakeside Jacuzzi halfway up the side of a mountain. While we don't *need* to, escaping our everyday lives can kick-start a Zen lifestyle the way Barry White can kick-start a first date. Things start to click just a little bit faster . . .

Look within. You are the Buddha.

Pretty much every step to finding bliss described in this book involves breaking old, convoluted patterns of thinking and replacing them with new habits that allow us to see things, people, and situations as they really are. But, as we all know, this kind of change is *hard*, and is especially difficult when everything around us stays the same, tempting us at every turn to fall right back into our old routines. So while we have the ability to transform ourselves without moving an inch, it doesn't hurt to step outside the familiar landscape of our normal lives and benefit from the jolt of being someplace totally new.

If you can afford the ticket, make your next vacation destination as foreign as possible. Heading for countries where we don't know the language or customs can have a wonderful effect on our thought processes, as it allows fewer assumptions to cloud the information we are taking in. We may step off the plane expecting to find a sign or a person telling us where to get our visa stamped, or stand on the curb expecting that there will be transportation options available, even it it's just one guy asleep at the wheel of a beat-up taxi. But, if we've gone someplace truly gutsy, where our expectations will be forced to take a backseat—no one in the airport speaks English, there isn't a taxi to be found—we begin to live in the moment and take things as they come.

Most people equate Buddhist-inspired travel with backpacks, blond dreadlocks, and the kind of b.o. that makes your eyes water, but roughing it is only one way to travel that can challenge your habitual thoughts and behaviors. It's perfectly possible to go the posh route while still exposing yourself to plenty of the unknown. The trick is to seek out finer things that are still mostly unfamiliar to you. Choose nicer hotels and restaurants that are geared toward natives rather than tourists. If you go on a tour, pick a guide who is from the area. When you're shopping, buy the clothes and products that the locals use from stores that don't have every label translated into English. The point isn't to make things difficult, it's to pay attention to the details, to entertain a broader range of possibilities, to ask questions. What's in that green bottle? Where will this bus take us? How do we use the bathroom when there's a bucket of water next to the toilet instead of a roll of toilet paper? We start to get used to the idea that we can't take anything for granted. And as we experience one inevitable mistake and misunderstanding after another, we start to get used to that, too. After every screw-up, bouncing back gets easier and easier. Eventually, all the ups and downs become part of the adventure.

· · · · · · · ·

Mini-Meditation: It's All in Your Head

Most of the time we forget that everything we experience only officially happens when it registers in our minds. Whether we're seeing, hearing, feeling, smelling, tasting, or touching, it all gets processed in our brains. Every memory that we have is limited to what our eyes were able to see, what our ears could hear, what we chose to touch or accidentally came in contact with, what we ate or drank, what scents we happened to encounter, and what we were thinking at the time. Consider how fragmented your knowledge of the world really is. Consider all that you haven't experienced. Imagine scenes that might be taking place in other countries and cultures right this minute. Even what you imagine is limited to piecing together what you already know, to form new images and ideas. After playing with these ideas a little, make a promise to yourself to try to absorb more information every time you look, hear, taste, touch, and smell something. To experience as much as possible, whether pleasant or unpleasant. To become more aware of the world around you.

Trekking halfway around the planet to spend time amid a culture that functions differently from our own is guaranteed to shake up our habitual MO, but a perspective-changing experience doesn't have to involve a passport. Chances are that within a day or two's drive, there's a city or a community where people live out of step with the fast-paced, modern life we call normal. Maybe it's a working ranch where you can ride a horse and help round up cattle; a vineyard that lets you spend all day picking grapes and all night drinking wine; an Amish town with no electricity; a hippie hot spring resort where everyone runs around naked. Even for one night, you could venture into a Goth club if that's never been your scene, attend a poetry reading, hit a cheesy disco, go roller-skating on gay night, go to a Star Trek convention, try a sport you've never played, attend a black-tie charity ball, anything that feels fresh or bizarre in your book. Go somewhere, anywhere that will surprise you, challenge you, throw you for a loop, and you're bound to regain a little open-minded curiosity, a little playfulness, and a little more willingness to let go of your urge to predict what comes next.

LEGGO YOUR EGO

A big part of going on a Zen vacation is to not plan it as thoroughly as you have trips in the past. Keep your research to essentials like transportation, lodging, and some basic information about what's available to do and see. If you're already the type who buys a plane ticket, shows up, and plays everything by ear, fantastic—you're a step ahead of the game. If, like me, you love to spend hours poring over guidebooks and Web sites in an attempt to guarantee an ideal experience, then it's time to curb that urge to bend the future to your will. As I've learned over and over again, excessive planning only leads to excessive disappointment. And it causes us to miss out on all sorts of opportunities that might arise out of nowhere.

Go Solo

If you haven't taken a trip on your own, you *must*. Do it now, before you have kids, before you can't afford it, before you have any more excuses than you have already. Traveling alone gives you a chance to understand who you are when you're not playing the role of a sister, friend, girlfriend, wife, coworker, or whatever role you play in everyday life. This can be an intimidating experience because, as in meditation, you start to realize that who you are, and what you think and feel, is more ambiguous and difficult to grasp than most people make it out to be. Without anyone around to please, or to agree or disagree with, and no work obligations, you become quiet inside and out.

For the first several days, being alone in a new place feels uncomfortable. It's boring. Things that should be fun feel pointless when you don't have someone to share them with. But then you realize that if you don't figure out how to enjoy yourself, you'll be wasting your time and money. So you decide to have a good time. And then . . . you do. You go out, meet new people, see new things, and start to enjoy yourself. And the idea that you have to depend on the people you care about to entertain you, to take care of you, to keep you sane, to make things matter, begins to lose some ground. You don't need them so much after all. You have them, and they're wonderful, but you can also exist all by yourself and find happiness on your own, no matter where you are or who you're with. The security and confidence that this knowledge provides is nothing less than life-changing. It inspires you to go back to your normal routine with a new strength and freedom, because you can now enjoy your connections with people without constantly worrying what would happen to you if it all were to change.

Even as I write these words and know that they're true, I'm always reluctant to follow this kind of play-it-by-ear advice. I love the new and unfamiliar because it's exciting, but it also makes me insecure and self-conscious. Traveling, although I do it all the time, gives me hives. On unfamiliar ground, we often end up standing around awkwardly, not knowing what to do next. Which is anything but relaxing. Our egos don't like being unsure of how the game is played in a given situation. We'd rather be the person sitting comfortably in our usual surroundings, feeling bad for the clueless, confused people wandering around trying to figure things out. When we do allow ourselves to be a little vulnerable, to ask other people for help, to fumble, we're defeating our egos in an extremely beneficial way. The human ego is often what blocks our ability to be compassionate and generous when a difficult situation comes up. The Buddhist concept of *anatta*, or selflessness, is rooted in the fact that when we stop worrying about protecting our self-image all the time, we become better, easier-going people. If a person insults us and we feel a strong urge to defend our ourselves, we get our revenge by insulting her right back. And if we have a strong attachment to our possessions, when someone damages something we own, we want to return the damage. In extreme cases, it's this very same ego-protecting instinct that causes violence and all-out war.

But we shouldn't confuse a well-padded ego with wimpy pacifism. A Buddhist isn't a doormat who will let anyone do anything to her or in front of her without interfering, but she is highly likely to bear small offenses without retaliating. The Dalai Lama advises that when someone criticizes us we should take it as an opportunity to increase our humility, whether we agree with the person's opinion or not. We're not perfect. We have flaws. We can actually, he says, feel gratitude toward them for reminding us of our fallibility and motivating us to improve. But the Dalai Lama also says that if someone tries to hurts us physically, we should definitely fight back with all we've got.

As a beginning traveler, or a rookie of any kind, we practice building our ego's resilience. Every time we go out on a limb by allowing ourselves to be insecure, our egos become a little less easily bruised. We stop caring if other people think they have one up on us, because we know it takes a lot more strength and courage to be voluntarily clueless than it does to stay huddled in our cocoon, pointing and snickering from a risk-free vantage point. As we venture beyond our comfort zones, we learn more about the world, our understanding of existence grows, we become more open-minded, and our lives are infinitely richer in color, sound, texture, smell, taste, and memory.

Get Your Relaxation On

For all my talk about heading out into the great unknown, going someplace that's designed to provide an atmosphere of quiet contemplation surrounded by natural beauty is an excellent way to start a meditation practice, or just reflect mindfully on your life.

Thanks to the popularity of spas and yoga, resorts have sprung up all over the country that emphasize soulful self-pampering. Of the many that I've had the good fortune to visit (reduced media rates were an awesome perk of being a magazine editor), those below stood out as especially peaceful, because of their location, lack of pretension, talented staff, and genuine dedication to Zen values (though none of them are officially Buddhist). Check out their Web sites to learn more.

Maya Tulum Resort (www.mayatulum.com) in Tulum, Mexico, consists of a rustic but luxurious-looking and feeling collection of thatched-roof huts on a gorgeous private beach (plus miles more to walk along in either direction). You'll find warm, turquoise waters, sand so fine and white it looks like baby powder, delicious and healthy food, a full bar, yoga classes every day, nearby ruins, and a huge nature reserve to explore. As you sit and sip Coronas in the dining hut (with a high thatched roof decorated with dozens of real silver lamps in the shape of stars), you see countless shades of blue through massive open windows that look out onto the sea and sky. The retreat itself is relatively inexpensive, as is getting there, since you can fly from Cancún and then take the bus.

Bishop's Lodge Resort and Spa (www.bishopslodge.com) in Sante Fe, New Mexico, is extremely posh, but it was built with so much respect and regard for nature that it feels very earthy and low-key. Wood for your fireplace is stacked neatly outside the door of your suite. Deer wander past your windows. You're highly likely to spot a bear cub eating berries out of a tree near the reception area. There are even horses there that you can rent for trail rides over brush-spotted hills and through rust-colored ravines. And if you're looking for proof that Georgia O'Keeffe sunsets are for real, look no further.

Gold Lake Mountain Resort and Spa (www.goldlake.com) in Ward, Colorado, is surrounded by mountain air so clean you feel like your lungs are being scrubbed with a toothbrush every time you inhale. Snowcapped mountains are visible in the distance as you look out over the lake, which is surrounded by beautiful pines and firs (at least that's what I thought they were). Again, the cabins make you feel like you're all alone in the wilderness, but they're stocked with two-foot-thick down comforters, wood burning fireplaces, and antique furniture that's probably worth a fortune. The ultimate feature of this ultra-relaxing spot up in the mountains above Boulder is the hot tubs tucked into the side of the hill facing the lake. They're made out of natural stone and fit so well into the landscape it's as if they were always there. Each one is placed so that it feels secluded and private. At night you can soak naked in the steaming water and then run down and jump in the cold lake that sparkles from the reflection of the moonlight on the rippling surface.

Hawk Inn and Mountain Resort (www.hawkresort.com) in Plymouth, Vermont, must be a place where the rich and famous come to play on the sly. The Inn at Hawk Resort is a charming, upscale place with a beautiful outdoor pool and acres and acres of forest-covered mountains to hike through. But the real jewels of this place are the Forest Preserve Lodges you can rent. These cabins have everything a woods-loving, spoiled star could want—Jacuzzi on the secluded porch, multiple fireplaces, skylights, flat-screen plasma TV, full kitchens well-enough equipped to satisfy a gourmet chef, and an invisible staff that materializes at the touch of a button. This place offers a rare combination of privacy and pampering that's worth the price, even if it's just for one or two nights. Two major ski resorts are a short drive away.

SEE BEYOND BEAUTY

Once you're on your way, try to keep your eyes open to both the pleasant and unpleasant things unfolding in front of you. A friend of mine who went to India on a tour of temples and palaces in an air-conditioned, first-class bus that promised to shield her from the overwhelming crush of crowds and the ubiquitous dust, was coaxed into visiting Varanasi, a holy city on the Ganges River where many Hindus go to perform purifying rituals. Because it is said that anyone whose ashes are scattered in the river will be blessed, many also go to Varanasi to die. Ceremonial funerals in which bodies are cremated on the riverbanks can be seen from dawn to dusk. When my friend returned from her trip, it was the images of sick and dying people on the streets and the sight and smell of burning flesh that stayed with her more than anything else. She considers it the most important thing she has ever witnessed because the memory fills her with a deep and instant appreciation for being alive and healthy. Much of the time, the profound is something beautiful, but almost as often it's something very difficult to look at or experience. Not turning your back when you encounter the gritty realism of life is probably the most valuable new Zen habit you can start forming as you travel. As in meditation practice, the idea is to acknowledge things as they are, without trying to resist them, so that we can respond to them intelligently and compassionately.

. . . .

Meditation en Masse

You may not know it, but there are probably half a dozen meditation groups within an hour of where you live, if not more. Most Buddhists don't wear any tell-tale signs of their beliefs, or try to recruit other people to join their sangha. It is understood that meditation is the kind of thing people seek out when they're ready and willing. If you're thinking about checking out a Buddhist lecture or meditation class, expect to find a room full of diverse people of all ages. The only generalization about the crowd at Buddhist events that I can *safely make is that most are well-educated and liberal. They're also extremely welcoming. Almost all teachers will address new people before they do anything else, and they always reemphasize the basics before moving on to discuss a specific topic in depth. The structure of a class is simple: after everyone finds a chair or cushion to sit on and the teacher gives a lecture about some aspect of Buddhism. This is followed by a guided meditation. Or sometimes the meditation will come first. I don't particularly like group activities, but I find it easier to meditate on a regular basis if I attend a scheduled class—not because it's any different from doing it alone, but because I'm lazy and need the peer pressure to stay still.*

LESS FEAR, MORE TRUST

A very important thing that travel can teach us is that we're a lot stronger and more capable than we might think. At home we can make intelligent guesses about what's likely to go wrong, and successfully prevent those things from happening. But in a place we've never been before, dangerous things can and do happen. Like the time a friend of my ex-boyfriend's developed a red lump on his face while traveling through Bolivia that turned out to be the developing eggs of a fly that had laid them there weeks ago while he was sleeping. And then there was the time my taxi driver in Kenya decided to drive alongside the highway instead of on it and ended up crashing head-on into a telephone pole, sending me and the other passenger to the emergency room in Nairobi. The truth of the matter is, surviving these experiences is surprisingly exhilarating. Instead of feeling timid, you become confident that you can take whatever the world throws at you. And if you can't handle something alone, you begin to have faith that someone *will* help you. With so many horrible things in the news every day, we forget that most people are like you and me—more than willing to lend someone a hand. When's the last time you said "No" when someone asked you for directions, or failed to help when someone fell or was hurt? That basic goodness exists all over the world. Getting into scrapes has the extremely positive side-effect of boosting your faith in the human race. For every person out there who wants to steal your wallet, you learn that there are three dozen who want to help you get it back.

❧

Monks Gone Wild: Tattoo Fever

Every year the Thai Buddhist temple of Wat Bang Phra, located thirty miles west of Bangkok, hosts a festival dedicated to the protective animal spirits that the monks and rice farmers in the area have worshipped and feared for generations, especially that of the fierce tiger. Some monks and men buy amulets to ward away evil, but the most powerful protection comes in the form of a tattoo administered by one of the temple's trained monks. Using a long, double-pronged needle dipped into a secret ink made of dye, herbs, and snake venom, the skin is stabbed quickly and repeatedly to embed the ink and create the design. Monks and laypeople from all over Thailand come to have their skin permanently marked with the temple's signature tiger or with carefully chosen lines from ancient prayers, and body art enthusiasts everywhere consider the festival to be one of the last sources of authentic tattooing in the world.

❧

When we're far away from home we need a way of reminding ourselves that the more relaxed and open we are to whatever may happen, the happier we'll be. Try using the mantra, "Just being here is cool enough," then kick back and take it easy. You can do it. It's like a gut instinct that gets buried under all of the pressure and stress of work and relationships but asserts itself the second we're able to step back and breathe. That inherent knowledge that every second that passes—whether exhilarating or boring, soothing or irritating, comfortable or painful, beautiful or ugly—is worthwhile simply because we're here, experiencing it, is at the heart of Buddhism and is the key to happiness. All we have to do is keep stepping back, breathing, and giving ourselves a chance to remember that it's true.

~ What to Read When . . . ~

. . . something central to your life—your relationship, your job, a member of your family, your home—is in crisis, or gone forever: *When Things Fall Apart* by Pema Chödrön. If your heart is broken, this book will help you.

. . . you're interested in the Buddhist idea that we don't need to be sure of any specific details about God in order to live a meaningful, compassionate life: *Buddhism Without Beliefs* by Stephen Batchelor. Batchelor explains why being comfortable with the idea that there are questions about life that have no answers is the most liberating way to live.

. . . you're starting to meditate and need a good coach: *A Gradual Awakening* by Stephen Levine. This unassuming guide acknowledges all of the little glitches that come up when we sit down and try to clear our minds, and gives gentle advice on how to stick with it.

. . . you're looking for a no-holds-barred confession from a punk rocker who overcame drug addiction and depression by studying Buddhism: *Dharma Punx* by Noah Levine. Son of author Stephen, Noah was suicidal by the age of five. Now he's a compassionate meditation teacher and therapist who still takes his music hard and fast.

. . . you want to read more of the words that came from the mouth of Buddha himself: *Teachings of the Buddha*, edited by Jack Kornfield. Carefully chosen passages from the most authoritative and clearly translated transcripts of Buddha's lectures help shed light on every aspect of the Dharma.

. . . you're curious about the actual life of Siddhartha Gautama on his path to becoming an enlightened being, and enjoy stories that involve a little magic: *The Life of the Buddha* by Bhikkhu Ñanamoli. This book tells the story of the Buddha's

life according to the Pali canon, starting from the moment he
came out of his mother's womb walking and talking until he
attained final nirvana, which caused "a great earthquake, fearful and hair-raising, and the drums of heaven resounded."

. . . you want to learn about the life of Buddha as told by a
practical-minded Buddhist nun who thinks ordinary life is
miraculous enough: *The Naked Buddha* by Venerable Adrienne Howley. This is one of my favorite books about Buddhism. In it, Howley answers all of the big questions about
Buddhism with astounding clarity. She's like a no-nonsense
grandma tellin' you what's up.

. . . you're wondering what young Western Buddhists' lives are
actually like on a day-to-day basis: *Blue Jean Buddha*, edited
by Sumi D. Loundon. This is a collection of essays by practicing
Buddhists who party, own iPods, and have one-night stands.

. . . you're interested in psychotherapy with a Buddhist twist:
Going to Pieces without Falling Apart by Mark Epstein, MD. If
you prefer getting guidance from someone whose academic
background is as strong as his spiritual one, Dr. Epstein is your
man. He seamlessly connects classic psychoanalytic theories
with Buddhist ideas.

. . . you want to put a gorgeous book of Buddhist-themed
photography on your coffee table or next to your bed to dip
into anytime: For a grand visual overview of Tibetan Buddhism,
Lillian Too's *The Buddha Book* offers page after oversized page
of gorgeous eye-candy. A smaller-scale, more personal option
is Steve McCurry's *The Path to Buddha*. He's the photographer
famous for that *National Geographic* cover portrait of the Afghani
girl with the intense green eyes (it appeared on the June, 1985
issue), and the images in this book are no less captivating.

GLOSSARY

Bodhicitta (bow-dee-chee-ta)—A deep compassion for all living, feeling things. Buddhists try to nurture their inner bodhicitta.

Buddha—An "awakened one," or person who is so fully aware of the nature of reality that he or she no longer feels the suffering caused by attachments or desire. Because he is the most famous of all buddhas, Siddhartha Gautama is known as "The Buddha," or simply as "Buddha."

Dharma (dahr-ma)—The wise and compassionate way of life prescribed by the teachings of Buddha. When a Buddhist follows the eightfold path, he is "practicing the dharma."

Karma (kahr-ma)—Universal karma is the law of cause and effect that dictates that wise, skillful behavior leads to happiness, and ignorant, unskillful behavior leads to suffering. An individual's "karma" is the present culmination of all the wise and unwise things they've done in the past.

Lama (lah-ma)—The Tibetan Buddhist term for a spiritual teacher.

(Tibetan Buddhists call their spiritual leader the Dalai Lama. "Dalai" means ocean. Together, Dalai Lama means "Ocean of Wisdom.")

Mantra (mahn-tra)—Harmonious syllables that are repeated in order to help quiet and focus the mind.

Nirvana (nerv-ah-na)—A state of bliss, profound inner peace, limitless awareness, and unity with all sentient beings. When a person attains nirvana, she accepts the true nature of suffering and so is no longer vulnerable to it.

Samsara (sahm-sah-ra)—A state of restlessness, dissatisfaction, suffering, desire, and non-awareness. Samsara is the opposite of nirvana.

Sattva (saht-tva)—A sentient being or living creature that has enough awareness to experience feelings such as pleasure and pain. Animals, fish, and even insects are considered sattvas; plants and mollusks like scallops and oysters are not.

Suttra (sue-tra)—A lesson or truth that is believed to have been stated by Buddha himself.

Tao (dow)—Similar to Buddhism, the ancient Chinese religious system called Taoism is based on the theory that everything in the universe is connected and constantly in flux. This truth is called the "Tao," and the way in which a person can live in harmony with this truth is also called the "Tao."

Zen—A Japanese school of Buddhism that focuses solely on meditation as a means of attaining wisdom. The word Zen has become synonymous with "calm," "peaceful," and "balanced."

Zendo (zen-doe)—A tranquil room used for group meditation by Zen Buddhists. A Zendo will usually be under the leadership of a single teacher called a Zen master, who will help students contemplate esoteric Buddhist concepts such as "Form is emptiness. Emptiness is form."

SOURCES

Pages 84 and 92, *"Angutta Nikaya,"* from Gil Fronsdale (trans.), *Teachings of the Buddha*. Revised and expanded edition. Edited by Jack Kornfield. Boston: Shambhala, 1996.

Page 41, *"Bhadekkaratta Sutta,"* from Thich Nhat Hanh, *Our Appointment with Life: The Buddha's Teachings on Living in the Present*. Berkeley, Calif.: Parallax Press, 1990.

Pages 51 and 69, *"Dhammapadda,"* from Thomas Byrom (trans.), *The Dhammapada: The Sayings of the Buddha*. New York: Knopf, 1976.

Teachings of the Buddha. Edited by Jack Kornfield with Gil Fronsdale. Boston: Shambhala, 1996.

ABOUT THE AUTHOR

Nicole Beland writes *Men's Health* magazine's monthly sex and relationship advice column "Ask the Girl Next Door," and is the author of the books *Ask the Men's Health Girl Next Door* and *The Cocktail Jungle: A Girl's Field Guide to Shaking and Stirring.* She lives in Brooklyn, New York.